Making Mortal Choices

Making Mortal Choices

Three Exercises in Moral Casuistry

Hugo Adam Bedau

New York Oxford
Oxford University Press
1997

Oxford University Press

Oxford New York
Athens Auckland Bangkok Bogota Bombay Buenos Aires
Calcutta Cape Town Dar es Salaam Delhi Florence Hong Kong
Istanbul Karachi Kuala Lumpur Madras Madrid Melbourne
Mexico City Nairobi Paris Singapore Taipei Tokyo Toronto

and associated companies in
Berlin Ibadan

Published by Oxford University Press, Inc.
198 Madison Avenue, New York, New York 10016

Oxford is a registered trademark of Oxford University Press

Library of Congress Cataloging-in-Publication Data
Bedau, Hugo Adam.
Making mortal choices : three exercises in moral casuistry /
Hugo Adam Bedau.
p. cm.
Includes bibliographical references and index.
ISBN 0-19-510877-9; ISBN 0-19-510878-7 (pbk.)
1. Casuistry. 2. Decision-making (Ethics)—Case studies.
I. Title.
BJ1441.B43 1996
170—DC20 96-16326

1 3 5 7 9 8 6 4 2

Printed in the United States of America
on acid-free paper

Preface

In the spring of 1994 I had the good fortune to be elected the eleventh Romanell-Phi Beta Kappa Professor of Philosophy, an award that carried with it the responsibility to offer three lectures of general interest to the Tufts University community. The three lectures were duly (but I hope not dully) given in the spring of 1995 under the collective title "Tragic Choices." They are published here essentially as they were originally delivered; only minor alterations—the deletion of some phraseology appropriate for lectures but unnecessary here, and the addition of an occasional explanatory or clarifying comment—have been made. As originally written, each lecture was intended to stand alone, without reliance on what went before or would come later; some repetition was the result, and not all such passages have been deleted or rewritten. Although there is, of course, more to be said (and probably some to be unsaid), I have not undertaken to rethink or elaborate at greater length my discussion of the issues beyond the way they were developed in the lectures.

I have subtitled this book *Three Exercises in Moral Casuistry* because it seemed to me appropriate to link what I have written to the casuistic tradition in western moral philosophy that stretches back more than two thousand years to the post-Aristotelians. Casuistry, as I explain at greater length in the appendix, is a part of practical (as opposed to theoretical, or meta) ethics; its distinctive methodological style requires focusing on particular cases (genuine or hypothetical). Each such case is, typically, vexatious and recalcitrant to obvious solution; the central questions it poses, "What ought one to do in this case and why?", are not easily answered. The cases discussed in this book are also momentous, involving life-and-death decisions. Hence the title for this book: *Making Mortal Choices*. (The lecture series title was not, on reflection, entirely appropriate. None of the cases I discuss is, strictly speaking, tragic.)

Not every mortal choice, however, presents us with a case for casuistry. William Styron's novel *Sophie's Choice* might seem to do so: Sophie has two children whom she loves equally. The Nazi officer at the gates to Auschwitz tell her she may choose one to be saved—but the other must be left to be murdered. Which of her two children ought Sophie to save? Her decision is certainly a momentous one. Yet her dilemma does not present us with a problem in casuistry. The reason it doesn't is that there are no *moral* grounds, reasons, or considerations relevant to the choice she must make in the circumstances. She loves her two children equally and there is no basis whatever on which she can choose between them, much less any time to deliberate. We cannot offer her any ethical counsel or considerations to improve (as one might put it) the ethical aspects of her decision making. The life-and-death choices discussed in this book, by contrast, are subject to much informed deliberation in which moral considerations are paramount, as will become evident.

Another distinctive feature of the cases I discuss and of the casuistry they invite is that the strategy for their solution is never top-down, deducing a solution by applying a general moral theory or a single moral principle. For this reason it can be misleading to describe casuistry, as is often done, as a species of applied ethics; "applied ethics" makes it sound if all that needs to be done is to apply an ethical principle to a particular case and then act accordingly. Casuistry, however, is more nearly the reverse, a kind of bottom-up strategy. Better still, to shift the metaphor, casuistry is a multiple triangulation of the region in which the best answer lies, the parameters or boundaries of the region being determined by the relevant ethical principles. One thus attempts to find the best advice for the decision maker by canvassing a wide range of possibilities, no one of which is dispositive—no one of which zeros in precisely on the target. The principles in question and the counsel they provide (given the facts of the case) emerge, bit by bit, at various stages of the analysis. For ease of reference and subsequent reflection, I have appended to each chapter a list of the moral principles identified and, in most cases, used in one way or another during the course of my discussion.

For three centuries casuistry has had a bad odor about it, because it seemed to its critics all too plainly to be a cynical and sophistical strategy to permit one to do whatever one wanted to do—it all depended on how ingenious one was in thinking up a subtle principle to yield the result one had antecedently made up one's mind to vindicate. This was once my view, too; however, it is not how I understand the enterprise now. The conclusions I reach in each of the three cases discussed in the chapters that follow were far from fixed in my mind at the start, even though I have discussed these cases with students over many years. Rather, the casuistic method as I practice it here is a way to investigate a case in which several moral problems turn out to be nested and intertwined with each other, and to do so without having independently any strong intuitions about how the issues should be resolved (much less any particular desire to vindicate one rather than another outcome). No doubt the casuistic method relies on moral intuitions of various sorts, but these intuitions do not necessarily prejudice the discussion or its outcome. (It is not, after all, as though we could or should try to approach moral problems devoid of convictions about what is wrong, a violation of someone's rights, unfair, or harmful.) And the particular circumstances of each case help us see the decisiveness of the relevant principles where they are decisive.

At the end of the book in the notes, I have added information on the sources I have used for the three cases I discuss and the writings of others from which I quote or to which I refer. I have also mentioned in the notes, here and there, other sources that are relevant to the topics under discussion, for readers sufficiently interested to want to explore some of the issues raised in greater detail. These references, however, only scratch the surface of a very large literature in contemporary normative ethics.

So much by way of preliminary comments. It remains only to thank those who made the original lectures and their publication possible: my colleagues in the Tufts chapter of Phi Beta Kappa who nominated me, and the scholars on the board of the national office of Phi Beta Kappa who elected me, to the Romanell professorship; Peter Hodgkinson, who arranged my visiting appointment on the law faculty of the University of Westminster (London) in the autumn of 1994, where these lectures were drafted; audiences at Westminster and the Institute for Advanced Legal Studies (London), who heard earlier versions of two of the three lectures and helped me to see my way toward improvements; the staff of the Tufts Department of Philosophy, whose arrangements and attention to detail made the lectures go smoothly; Norman Daniels, who urged me to seek publication for the lectures, and my other departmental colleagues, whose support has been gratifying and encouraging; Priscilla Taylor, editor of *The Key Reporter,* where a much-abbreviated version of my third lecture was published in the Winter 1995–96 issue; the publisher and editors of *The Encyclopedia of Ethics,* Garland Press, 1992, from which my essay on casuistry is reprinted; my editor at Oxford University Press, Cynthia Read, and the two anonymous readers of my lectures for the press; and, first and last, my wife, Constance Putnam, whose sharp eye has once again saved me from many errors and infelicities in the spoken and written word. To all these my thanks and gratitude.

Concord, Massachusetts H. A. B.
September 1996

Contents

Making Mortal Choices

ONE

Seaman Holmes and the Sinking of the William Brown

I

At about 10 o'clock on the cold, wet night of April 19, 1841, in the North Atlantic some 250 miles southeast of Cape Race in Newfoundland, the Philadelphia-bound frigate *William Brown* struck an iceberg. Those on board—65 Scots and Irish emigrants and a crew of 17 including 3 officers—were in immediate peril of their lives. The *William Brown* carried only two lifeboats, a so-called jolly-boat that could safely hold 10 and a longboat adequate for perhaps two dozen. The captain, the second mate, six crewmen, and two passengers (a woman and a boy) quickly filled the smaller boat. Into the larger boat clambered the first mate, eight crewmen, and 32 passengers—far more than the boat could safely hold. Left on board with no hope of survival were the remaining 31 passengers; within an hour and a half of the collision, the ship went down and they drowned.

As dawn turned into morning the two lifeboats with their

exhausted and terrified survivors began to drift apart, but not before the captain in the jolly-boat ordered the crew in the longboat to obey the first mate just as they would him. The first mate, for his part, reported to the captain that in his judgment the longboat was (in the words used later by the court reporter) "unmanageable"—the rudder was broken, water was leaking in through various holes, and the gunwales of the overloaded boat were dangerously near the water. If the boat were to have any chance of staying afloat, "it would be necessary to cast lots and throw some overboard" (again, I quote the court reporter's words). The captain (as later court testimony established) replied, calling across the water, "I know what you'll have to do. . . . Don't speak of that now. Let it be the last resort." With that, the two boats parted company.

The weather turned foul during the day; rain fell steadily, and in the longboat the passengers struggled to bail the water while the crew worked the oars. But by 10 in the evening, just twenty-four hours after the collision with the iceberg (again, in the words of the court reporter), "the wind began to freshen, the sea grew heavier, and once, or oftener, the waves splashed over the boat's bow so as to wet, all over, the passengers. . . . Pieces of ice were still floating around, and . . . icebergs had been seen. . . . [T]he rain falling rather heavily . . . and the boat having considerable water in it, the [first] mate, who had been bailing for some time, gave it up, explaining 'This work won't do. Help me, God. Men, go to work.' Some of the passengers cried out, about the same time: 'The boat is sinking. . . . God have mercy on our poor souls.' But the crew did not respond to the mate's order. A few minutes later, the mate shouted to the crew, 'Men, you must go to work, or we shall all perish.' They then went to work; and . . . before they ended, 14 male passengers, and also 2 women" were thrown overboard to certain death by drowning.

It appears from the court testimony of the survivors that the selection and casting overboard of the 14 men took many hours; the last two consigned to a watery grave were not dispatched until dawn. The weather improved and early in the morning the longboat with its remaining occupants were seen and rescued by a ship. The survivors in the jolly-boat were saved by another ship, but not until after they had spent six days and nights adrift on the high seas.

A year later, in 1842, in federal court in Philadelphia, one and only one member of the crew was indicted under the provisions of a federal statute to the effect that "the punishment for certain crimes against the United States" shall be imprisonment for not more than three years and a fine of not more than a thousand dollars. The crime in question was "manslaughter on the high seas" committed by any "seaman" or other person. In the aftermath of the sinking of the *William Brown,* the sole person charged under this statute was not the ship's captain, not the first mate, but a mere crewman, Alexander William Holmes by name.

Holmes was 26, Finnish by birth, a sailor since his youth, and—once more, in the words of the court reporter—with a "frame and countenance [that] would have made an artist's model for decision and strength." He was the last crew member to leave the sinking ship, having performed heroically in rescuing passengers who otherwise would have drowned trying to escape. While in the longboat he had given to the women on board "all his clothes except his shirt and pantaloons." It was he who spotted the rescue vessel, and thanks to "his exertions the ship was made to see, and finally to save them." At the trial, the captain testified that Holmes "was always obedient to officers. I never had a better man on board ship. He was a first rate man." And so he seems to have been.

II

So much for the facts. Let us begin by identifying the principle of selection on which the crew acted in deciding whom to throw overboard (this and other principles to be mentioned have been listed on p. 35). According to testimony in court, the first mate ordered the crew "not to part man and wife, and not to throw over any women." (Whether the two sisters who went overboard did so in a futile attempt to save their brother or out of despair over his imminent death was never resolved.) Evidently, the mate ignored his own earlier proposal to the captain, if proposal is what it was, to hold a lottery to determine who would be thrown over. Except for the mate's admonition about spouses and women mentioned above, the court reporter tells us, "[t]here was no other principle of selection. There was no evidence of combination among the crew [that is, no conspiracy to drown some passengers]. No lots were cast, nor had the passengers . . . been either informed or consulted as to what was [to be] done." The result of following the mate's order was that all the male passengers were thrown overboard except for two married men whose wives were in the longboat and a small boy.

So it looks as if the first mate's order and the crew's actions rested on a selection principle we might call *Save Families,*

Women, and Children. However, this is not so. For we also learn from the court reporter that "Not one of the crew was cast over"—which provoked the reporter to add, somewhat ominously, "One [of the crew], the cook, was a negro." The failure to cast out of the boat any of the crew cannot have been accidental; it must have been intentional. If so, it looks as if the crew interpreted—indeed, significantly revised—the selection principle implied by the mate's original order. Their conduct amounted to acting on a principle we might call *Save Families Plus Crew* (construing families here to include single women and children as well as married couples). We should note, however, that there is no evidence that the mate protested this interpretation or revision of his principle, and so it may well be that Save Families Plus Crew—below, I shall refer to this as the *operative selection principle*—did in fact express his unstated intention.

Why were Holmes and the other crew members willing to act on this principle? It is plausible to understand the first mate's order and the crew's compliance with it as their best judgment in the circumstances of how to achieve the goal of saving the most possible lives. The point of the selection principle was to achieve this goal. Other possible goals suggest themselves, admittedly, but the goal I shall call *Save the Most Possible* seems to me the right way to describe the end to which the mate's order and the operative principle were understood to be the means.

Another principle is also at work here. We cannot understand what Holmes and the other sailors did unless we grant that they were also acting in compliance with a principle we might call *Sailor's Duty to Obey Orders*. The mate, it will be recalled, told the crewmen to "go to work, or we shall all perish." Without some such direction from the mate, it is difficult to understand Holmes's behavior. At the trial (if we can trust the court reporter), no one suggested that Holmes took it upon himself to decide *when* to throw passengers overboard, or *whether* to throw them overboard, or even *whom* to throw overboard. We can reasonably suppose that if the first mate had ordered Holmes to act according to some other principle of selection, Holmes would have done so in the same resolute manner in which he acted on the operative selection principle.

The principle of Sailor's Duty to Obey Orders, understood as a principle of justification of questionable conduct, has its reciprocal in the *Defense of Superior Orders.* We know from the Nuremberg Trials in the 1940s and the My Lai court martials in the 1960s, as the court that tried Holmes also knew, that this defense cannot be invoked without careful qualification. But Seaman Holmes was no Gauleiter Julius Streicher, or even a Lieutenant William Calley. Crimes against humanity committed by those officers cannot be justified on the ground that they were merely carrying out superior orders. Even if they did not know that what they did was criminal, they should have known, for they had adequate time in the circumstances to reflect on their orders and sufficient intelligence and information to cause them to realize the nature of their deeds. Can we say as much of Holmes—that he, too, should have known the first mate's order was unlawful and immoral, assuming for the moment that it was? I do not think we can. To do so implies that Holmes had time to reflect on and weigh the mate's order, that a mere sailor ought to be able to tell the difference between a legitimate and an illegitimate order issued in the direst of circumstances, and that he ought to be able to decide whether to obey or disobey an order of doubtful legitimacy. These are unacceptable implications. So, even if we are inclined to judge the mate's order as unlawful and immoral, that would not suffice to find fault with Holmes for obeying it and interpreting it as he did.

III

We come now directly to the question of the legitimacy of the operative selection principle. The question divides into two parts: On what ground was *this* principle chosen over alternative selection principles? and On what ground was *any* principle of selection chosen? Let us address the second question first.

Much, even if not quite everything, in this case hinges on whether it really was *necessary* to cast anyone overboard. The question is obviously crucial, because if the answer is in the affirmative then there is a strong argument in support of what Holmes did. Not, to be sure, an argument wholly exonerating him, because it could still be objected that the wrong selection principle was used to determine who should be sacrificed—a point to which I shall return shortly. In any case, the question of the necessity with which Holmes acted cannot be answered straightaway, as though it were like the question, Is it necessary for a body unsupported in space to fall toward the earth's surface? or like the question, Is it necessary that every vixen is a female fox? For no natural law or semantic rule, as in these cases (respectively), governed the lives and deaths of those in the longboat. Any necessity for some in the boat to die was itself a contingent necessity, a necessity, that is, contingent on the prior acceptance of the goal of saving some lives and contingent on the absence of any other mode of flotation for those ousted from the longboat. So the question that needs to be answered here is, rather, this: Was it necessary for some to be cast overboard and thus to die by drowning so that others in the longboat could have an improved chance of survival?

The answer depends on two very different considerations. One is the facts of the matter, that is, the circumstances of the sea; the weather; and, especially, the condition of the longboat; and the beliefs about these matters held by the first mate, the crew, and the passengers. The other is the acceptability of the selection principle connecting the end of survival to the means of survival. At its most abstract, this principle of justification declares that if not all can survive and if the deaths of a few are a necessary (although not a sufficient) condition of the survival of many, then those deaths are justified. Let us call this the *Sole Means Necessary to the End* principle. What I have called the operative selection principle, Save Families Plus Crew, is just a mode of implementation of the much more fundamental principle of justification, the Sole Means Necessary to the End principle. Let us look more closely both at the facts and at this new principle.

First, the facts. Testimony in the court record on the condition of the sea, the weather, and the boat is not unambiguous; there is no certainty about the actual state of the weather and some uncertainty about just how bad the first mate, crew, and passengers thought the weather was. But put yourself for the moment in the soaking wet and bitterly cold shoes of the first mate in the longboat. You are in charge, and the lives of all turn on your judgment. You have no way of knowing whether the seas will worsen, perhaps rapidly, and no way of knowing whether the leaky boat will leak more extensively or how much more water over its bow and gunwales the overloaded boat will take on if the wind freshens, and how much more it can take on without becoming swamped. In acting on any principle of selection the margin of error is very slim indeed. Better to err on the safe side, if error there must be—or so the first mate may well have thought. And while it is true that within a few hours the weather did improve, it will forever remain uncertain whether the leaky and overcrowded longboat could have survived the half-dozen or so hours from 10 o'clock to dawn if the boat's load had not been lightened of some of its human cargo. Keeping in mind the perilous condition of everyone in the longboat, I think many would be ready to agree with me that it was necessary—or at least reasonable for experienced seamen to believe it was necessary—for some to get out of the boat if any in the boat were to have a chance of surviving the night.

If we reach such a judgment, however, we are sharply at odds with the court of law in which Holmes was tried. The prosecutor, George M. Dallas, argued that none of the homicides Holmes caused was necessary, and the trial judge, Circuit Justice Henry Baldwin, going by his charge to the jury, seems to have agreed. The law on the defense of necessity, according to Baldwin, requires that "[t]he peril must be instant, overwhelming, leaving no alternative but to lose our own life, or to take the life of another person." The clear but tacit implication of this remark was that the jury should conclude on the facts as shown that the defense of necessity should fail. And the jury eventually agreed, finding Holmes guilty of manslaughter as charged.

However, before we agree with the prosecutor, the judge, and the jury, we need to consider two objections to their view. By defining necessity as he did, Judge Baldwin seems to imply that if Holmes really had acted in necessity, he could not have acted on the principle he did act on, namely that of Save Families Plus Crew. Instead, the judge implies, Holmes would have had to act on a very different selection principle, one we might call *First Reached, First Overboard.* This is a better principle on which to act in the face of a "peril [that is] instant, overwhelming," and "leaving no alternative." Under this principle of selection, Holmes, and whichever fellow crewmen were handy, when threatened with imminent swamping in the overloaded boat pitching among the waves in the black of night, would have simply thrown over whomever they could reach first, not bothering about niceties of gender or marital status and not stopping to ascertain who was crew and who was passenger. So the fact that Holmes did not act on the principle of First Reached, First Overboard virtually proves that his defense of acting out of necessity ought to collapse. Or so this argument implies. This is reinforced if, as testimony in court alleged, the time from which the first person to the last was cast over the side was six hours or more.

One consequence of this reasoning is that Judge Baldwin must view the defense of necessity as an excuse for homicide, not a justification. One *excuses* oneself from blame for the harm one has done to another by conceding that it was wrong to cause the harm, but that nevertheless in the circumstances it couldn't be helped and that therefore one can't really be blamed for it. Thus, if one cannot help but strike out to save one's own life, circumstances preventing any deliberation and reflection, then one ought to be excused by the law. One *justifies* oneself for causing harm to another by showing that one did it deliberately and after due reflection, because in the circumstances it was the right (or the best) thing to do. Judge Baldwin in effect advised the jury that although there could be no justification for what Holmes did, he could be excused if he acted of necessity. But he couldn't be excused since he did not act of necessity, as necessity is defined in the law.

I do not find this reasoning convincing, any more than I find myself in agreement with the jury that there was no necessity facing those in the longboat to lighten the load as promptly as possible. As for the aspect of the argument that turns on the facts, I see no way to settle it to general satisfaction. It seems to me the mate must have believed the overloaded longboat faced danger from swamping at every minute; why else would he have ordered the crew to throw anyone overboard? And if it was reasonable for Holmes to believe the mate, who by hypothesis believed the danger of swamping was imminent, then it really doesn't matter whether swamping was imminent. Holmes, the first mate, and the rest of the crew in effect acted on the Sole Means Necessary to the End principle, and that principle, had they thought of it, would have assured them that the deaths they caused were justified by the even greater number of deaths their actions averted.

IV

Deferring for the present any closer scrutiny of that principle of justification, let us shift our attention to the operative selection principle, Save Families Plus Crew, and start by considering some alternatives to it. Consider first a scheme that might seem to obviate any need for a selection principle at all. This scheme requires us to distinguish between lightening the boat's load and throwing persons overboard to drown. Why not (so this scheme suggests) lighten the load by the expedient of everyone taking turns in the water? Surely, under the crew's supervision, a regular rotation could have been set up so that a dozen or so in the boat would climb out, hang on to the gunwales for half an hour, and then climb back in as others climbed out to take their turn in the cold water. Couldn't all have survived this way—or at least more than did survive? Shouldn't the necessity to lighten the longboat be kept distinct from any necessity for some to drown?

But trying to undermine the necessity for casting some overboard by appeal to a scheme of rotation in and out of the longboat stretches credulity to the breaking point; it is hopelessly unrealistic, and in this regard is like several other selection principles alternative to the operative principle.

To illustrate the point, let us consider two among the many such alternative principles. One we might call *Save the Best,* an elitist principle that tells us to protect from drowning those most fit among the passengers and crew, according to some criterion of fitness. The other principle is familiar from its applications in layoff and redundancy judgments, the principle of seniority, or *Last In, First Out.* Trying to act on either of these selection principles would certainly have proved completely unmanageable in the circumstances, for reasons I trust need not be spelled out. We must put them and other abstractly attractive but functionally futile principles entirely out of mind. In our judgment about relevant and appropriate principles, we must keep firmly before us the conditions of the boat and the weather, the terror of the passengers, the uncertain loyalties of the crew, and the apparent necessity of quickly lightening the human cargo in the longboat, even though doing so meant virtually certain death by drowning for those cast overboard. Whatever may in the end be said against the operative principle, one cannot object that it is not a feasible principle on which to act in pursuit of the goal Save the Most Possible.

Notice, by the way, a certain inescapable vagueness in the actual application of whatever selection principle is chosen. Given that some must exit the boat to certain death, no matter what principle of selection is chosen, the question remains, How many should be forced to do so? Why more than a dozen, 16, to be exact (or 14, if you prefer to believe the two sisters went overboard voluntarily)? Why not only 10? Or eight? Or six? We have no answer to this question. No hint of a reason is given for the decision—apparently Holmes's, as he interpreted the first mate's order, and as was at least acquiesced in by the mate—to throw overboard *all* the unmarried male passengers. Perhaps we may conjecture that Holmes and the first mate thought along these lines: First, to ensure that a real margin of safety for those remaining in the boat had been obtained by sacrificing some, it was desirable to sacrifice one or two more rather than one or two fewer, and, second, the only way to be fair to all the unmarried men was to not choose among them but to sacrifice them all. Not very convincing reasons, perhaps, but if there are better ones they have not occurred to me—any more than they apparently occurred to the mate or the crew.

V

Returning now to the operative principle, Save Families Plus Crew, we must notice that this principle—as well as any alternative to it on which Holmes might have acted—has a feature widely thought to condemn it as unfairly applied in such circumstances: Those who were to live and die by the application of the operative selection principle never consented to be judged by it. No agreement was signed by all the passengers when they boarded the ship that, were the ship to sink and necessity indicate the need to sacrifice some, they would be sacrificed according to the principle Save Families Plus Crew. Nor was any poll taken of the passengers in the longboat to see whether all subscribed to this principle. So one must wonder with what right the captain and the first mate gave orders to the crew to implement a principle that no one could be sure all the passengers accepted. Surely, some will say, it is no more up to the officers of the ship to decide what principle to act on than it is for the passengers to decide on their own.

Why might we insist on explicit unanimous consent to a principle of selection before it is applied? Because there is no other way to respect the equal rights of all the persons involved. No one has the right to use me as a means to the ends of others without my voluntary and informed consent, or so many philosophers have said, beginning with Kant—and for that reason I will call this the *Kantian Condition.* If we accept the Kantian Condition, we must reject the operative selection principle as applied in the longboat. More than that, if it is a necessary condition of justifiably applying a principle of selection that there be explicit unanimous consent to that principle, then no selection in the longboat was morally permissible. So we must also reject what I have called the principle of the Sole Means Necessary to the End, because that principle justifies the death of some when it is a necessary condition to the survival of others, whether or not they consent. Such a principle clearly flouts the Kantian Condition.

So we see that the first mate and the crew ignored the Kantian Condition. They acted on a principle of selection not knowing whether any, much less all, of those to whom it would be applied had consented to it. In so acting, they did what many would call violating the rights of others—albeit in a good cause. We can also say that the court, in trying Holmes for manslaughter, also ignored the Kantian Condition, as will become evident when we consider the court's somewhat equivocal endorsement of a lottery as the proper principle of selection.

Earlier, I said that if one accepts the Kantian Condition as a necessary constraint on any acceptable principle of selection, then no principle of selection is available to those in the longboat. That is a hard conclusion to accept. Perhaps we could evade it by arguing that the operative principle ought nevertheless to be accepted, for two reasons. First, it is a better principle than any competing principle in the circumstances, as we will see after identifying and evaluating the competing principles. Second, if all principles of selection are rejected, because all violate the Kantian Condition, that forces us to embrace what we might call the principle of *Shared Disaster*: Where not all can survive, although most could (or at least could have an increased likelihood of survival), but only at the expense of others, none of whom will volunteer for a sacrificial role, it is better for none to survive.

VI

To act on the principle of Shared Disaster, the first mate would have had to ask for volunteers to go overboard, and, getting no response, would then have had to inform everyone in the boat that since there were no volunteers, and since no one would be selected for being cast overboard without his or her consent to the principle of selection, and since there was no consent to any principle of selection, everyone should understand that under the prevailing conditions the boat would probably sink and all would drown, Amen. Obviously, Shared Disaster is not a principle of selection at all; rather, it is the default position when all principles of selection have been rejected.

In reflecting on this outcome, we need to ask, Is it better for those in the longboat to accept the Kantian Condition, thus rejecting all principles of selection in favor of the principle of Shared Disaster? Or is it better for them to act on some selection principle, because *any* such principle is better in its outcome than Shared Disaster? If the criterion for acceptance of a principle is whether it would be accepted unanimously behind a veil of ignorance (where one imagines oneself deprived of all knowledge about one's own circumstances, for example, one's age or sex or talents), then Shared Disaster is inferior to any selection principle. For anyone could see—not knowing whether he or she was a passenger or crewman, adult or child, male or female, married with spouse present or not—that one had no chance of survival under Shared Disaster, whereas there was some chance of survival under any selection principle—and, a fortiori, a chance under the operative principle. All would prefer some (not necessarily the same) selection principle over Shared Disaster, purely on grounds of self-interest. Of course, all this reasoning proves at best, it might be argued, is that if the choice among principles is to be based on self-interest behind a veil of ignorance, then it is clear which of these two principles would be chosen. But this fails to show which principle is the better, since it is always possible that the better principle is not the one chosen out of self-interest behind a veil of ignorance.

As an example of a selection principle that is arguably better in this context than either the operative principle or the principle of Shared Disaster—but not more likely to be chosen behind a veil of ignorance—consider the principle we might call *Self-sacrifice of the Weak*: Where many can survive only if not all survive, then it is best if the few who are weak, infirm, aged, or otherwise burdensome choose to sacrifice themselves for the survival of others. (Do not confuse the principle of Self-sacrifice of the Weak with another principle, *Sacrifice the Weak*; the latter is functionally equivalent to Save the Best, and is no more applicable here than that principle is.) Self-sacrifice of the Weak comes close to the principle on which Captain Titus Oates acted in 1910 in the Antarctic when, sick and, as he probably believed, dying, he crawled out of the snowbound tent shared with his fellow explorers into a roaring blizzard and did not return, thereby deliberately lightening the burden on his comrades and giving them a better chance of survival. Although his act proved futile (everyone on the expedition eventually perished anyway), to this day Oates is celebrated as a selfless hero. The esteem in which he has been held for nearly a century is strong evidence, if not proof positive, that the principle on which he acted is morally superior to all alternatives that would have had him acting otherwise (or acting as he did but for different reasons). (Notice, by the way, that Oates's sacrifice does not flout the Kantian Condition, since he chose to make the welfare of others his own end—that is, he chose to act in a manner that made his action a means to further the survival of others, an end he freely and knowingly endorsed.)

This ought to encourage us to say that if you grant the paramount importance of some in the longboat surviving and the proposition that not all can survive in the circumstances, then you ought to agree that the best of the relevant principles for selecting who shall die was not the principle on which the crew acted in carrying out the first mate's order. But we must also say that the principle of Self-sacrifice of the Weak, however excellent it may be, was not a principle, apparently, on which anyone in the longboat was prepared to act. This is proved by their actual conduct. And this suggests that we need to search for a second-best selection principle, one we hope those in the lifeboat could have agreed, in principle, to act on in the circumstances, even if in practice their agreement to this or any other principle could not be obtained. This brings us right back to the operative principle itself.

VII

Given that a few in the longboat must get out and drown if the rest are to survive, one may nevertheless doubt whether Save Families Plus Crew was the best principle of selection in the circumstances. Surely, for us today this principle suffers from an overly sentimental devotion to "family values." Worse than that, it seems selfish beyond belief to protect the crew from any risk of being sacrificed for the greater good, especially if some of the crew (such as the cook) were no more adept at handling a small boat than we can assume at least some of the single male passengers were. Why not act on a principle we might call *Equal Risk,* under which all in the longboat would have roughly equal risk of being thrown overboard? The way to have implemented that principle would have been by a fair and inclusive lottery, which was what the first mate, it will be recalled, had originally mentioned to the captain (although at the time he ignored it) before the two lifeboats separated. Surely, Equal Risk appears to be the principle most likely to withstand criticism for choice behind a veil of ignorance.

Perhaps not. In the case as reported to us, we hear no defense of the operative principle, Save Families Plus Crew. Speaking briefly on its behalf, I suggest it is defensible on three grounds. First, as to choosing only single male passengers, little or no problem arises in determining who in the lifeboat meets that description. So the principle is easy to apply consistently, although hardly uniquely so. Second, whereas a wife would be likely to come under the protection of her husband, and vice versa, no matter under what principle one spouse but not the other might have been chosen to be thrown overboard, no one in these circumstances was likely to come to the defense of a single male passenger. If, therefore, any were to be thrown overboard, it was best to throw overboard those most easily disposed of without interference, namely, the single male passengers. Finally, as to exempting the crew, is it not plausible to believe that without any crew there was little or no chance that any passengers would survive the unpredictable ordeal ahead? (No one could know that the ordeal would last only one night; recall that nearly a week passed before those in the jolly-boat were rescued.) To be sure, refusing for this reason to cast overboard all of the crew is not an argument for refusing to cast any of them overboard. Yet imagine the fight that might well have broken out among the crew had Holmes and one or two other crewmen tried to oust the rest of the sailors. Surely, avoiding such a struggle was in everyone's interest.

In sum, it may be excessive to say of the operative selection principle what defense counsel Edward Armstrong said when he described it as a "clear dictate of humanity" and "the only principle of selection which was possible in an emergency like theirs." But I would insist that Save Families Plus Crew is not bereft of reason, and that behind a veil of ignorance it might well triumph, after due reflection, even over Equal Risk as the best principle to apply in the circumstances. For the issue between the two principles, Equal Risk and Save Families Plus Crew, is this: Would you prefer a greater chance of staying in the longboat (offered by Equal Risk) or a greater chance of survival if you are lucky enough to remain in the longboat (offered by Save Families Plus Crew)?

VIII

The prosecution and the court, however, looked at the choice among selection principles very differently. Dallas, the prosecutor, in effect insisted on two major points. He argued, first, that several considerations governed the behavior of those in the longboat: the paramount goal of *Passenger's Safety First,* the principle of *Sailor's Duty of Self-sacrifice,* and the principle of Equal Risk. Second, Dallas implied that Holmes had violated all three. Let us look more closely at his arguments.

First, he argued that it was contrary to all the rules of the sea for the crew to be immune from fatal risk, as they were under the operative principle. "We protest," he declared, "against giving to seamen the power thus to make jettison of human beings, as of so much cargo; of allowing sailors, for their own safety, to throw overboard, whenever they may like, whomsoever they may choose. . . . The seaman, we hold, is bound, beyond the passenger, to encounter the perils of the sea. To the last extremity, to death itself, must he protect the passenger. It is his duty." The judge echoed these sentiments, saying in part, "The sailor is bound . . . to undergo whatever hazard is necessary to preserve the boat and the passengers. Should the emergency become so extreme as to call for the sacrifice of life, there can be no reason why the law does not still remain the same. The passenger, not being bound either to labour or to incur the risk of life, cannot be bound to sacrifice his existence to preserve the sailor's."

On this showing, it appears that only crew members should have been thrown overboard if any persons were to be thrown, or at least that all crew members would have to be cast over before any passengers. But there are two objections to this course of action. First, as we have seen, Holmes and the other crewmen clearly believed it was their duty to obey the orders of the first mate. Are we to think that in the circumstances they should have realized that their duty to the surviving passengers overrode their duty to obey the ship's officers? As for Passenger's Safety First, no one will dispute that it is of paramount importance. But it is not clear that this principle is violated by acting on the operative selection principle. After all, in acting as they did, the mate, Holmes, and the other crewmen managed to save the lives of 18 passengers, as well as their own. As for the principle of Sailor's Duty of Self-sacrifice, no doubt there is much to be said for it. Yet one must wonder whether, when Holmes heard it invoked by Judge Baldwin in open court, it was the first time he had heard of it.

Second, if Holmes and the rest of the crew, including the first mate, acted on the principle Sailor's Duty of Self-sacrifice, how would the longboat then have been handled, with none but terrified and inexperienced passengers left on board? Indeed, the goal of Passenger's Safety First, coupled with the goal of Saving the Most Possible, arguably required rejecting Sailor's Duty of Self-sacrifice in the circumstances. This obvious possibility was simply ignored by the prosecutor. Judge Baldwin, however, was more cautious; he rightly said that "The captain [for whom in this context read the first mate] . . . and a sufficient number of seamen to navigate the boat, must be preserved." But this proviso effectively nullifies any reliance on the principle of Sailor's Duty of Self-sacrifice in this case, since even if all and only the eight crew members and the first mate had been thrown overboard, that might not have been enough to give the rest the added margin of safety plausibly believed to be required in the circumstances. It would also have introduced a new element of risk for the passengers lucky enough to be in the longboat but unluckily now required to fend for themselves in turbulent seas.

IX

This may be a natural point at which to ask whether the passengers had a right to their seats in the longboat, such that throwing any of them overboard would violate their rights. Consider the issue more abstractly. Suppose there is exactly one life preserver or one vacant seat in a lifeboat, and two persons, a passenger and a crewman, claiming it. Which, if either, has a right to that life preserver or seat? Surely, in the absence of some special explanation, it is the passenger who has the right, exactly as Judge Baldwin implied. The principle discussed earlier, Sailor's Duty of Self-sacrifice, can be seen as a reflection of the fact that passengers have rights that entail duties for sailors, whereas passengers as such have no duties that arise from any rights of sailors.

But this is of little help in the context of our case. If any passengers have a right to sit in the longboat, then all do, and their rights are equal. Since in the longboat there was not enough space for all (and only) the passengers while maintaining the minimal margin of safety against swamping, the problem becomes one of fair allocation of seats among too many passengers with equal claims. Given the necessity to lighten the boat, some passengers or some crew must be thrown overboard. Accordingly, the prosecutor argued that if the principle of Sailor's Duty of Self-sacrifice proved unpersuasively demanding, then another principle of selection should have been used. "Common settlement," he said, "would . . . have fixed the principle of sacrifice, and, the mode of selecting involving all. . . . [A]t sea, sailor and passenger stand upon the same base, and in equal relations." In other words, the principle of selection should be Equal Risk and the method a fair lottery in which all would participate equally. Dallas did not connect his argument for a lottery to any claim of rights by the passengers, although he might well have done so. Again, however, Judge Baldwin was more cautious. He agreed with Dallas that, abstractly considered, that is, apart from circumstances, "selection . . . by lot . . . is resorted to as the fairest mode, and, in some sort, as an appeal to God, for selection of the victim." But unlike the prosecutor, the judge conceded that in the actual circumstances it might have been unreasonable or even impossible to contemplate selection by lottery. Perhaps this is what the first mate thought, too; for, as we have seen, he did not in the end propose any such lottery in the actual circumstances.

Surely Judge Baldwin was right. Defense counsel Armstrong put it more strongly: "[W]ho has ever told of casting lots at midnight, in a sinking boat, in the midst of darkness, of rain, of terror, and of confusion? To cast lots when all are going down, but to decide who shall be spared . . . is a plan easy to suggest, rather difficult to put in practice." Quite so. The principle of Equal Risk, like the alternative principles Save the Best and Last In, First Out, is simply not a feasible principle on which to act in order to sacrifice some lest none survive, all the while endeavoring to save the most possible in the circumstances.

Again, two interesting points suggest themselves. First, we might imagine getting around the difficulty of holding a lottery in the longboat by deciding instead to rely on a different kind of arbitrary principle of selection, one well known to the armies of ancient Rome: the principle of *Decimation*. Here's how it would have worked: By counting, the first mate determines that there are (for simplicity's sake, let us say) 36 people in the boat and that 12 must be thrown overboard. Accordingly, he instructs Holmes and two crewmen to throw overboard every third person, regardless of who it is. Such a selection principle has the same features of randomness and fairness that recommend a true lottery, but it is far easier to administer. Whether it could be both judged superior to the operative selection principle, and implemented in the circumstances as effectively as that principle, I will not pause to consider.

The court, however, perhaps owing to an excess of enthusiasm for the principle of Equal Risk, overlooked a point that friends of the Kantian Condition would not: However fair a selection by lottery may be, acting on the principle of Equal Risk is only marginally better than selection by any other principle as long as not all consent to decision by lottery. Since the court failed to give any weight at all to the Kantian Condition, its support for a lottery places the court among those who accept without qualms the principle of justification I previously called the Sole Means Necessary to the End.

As for the equal rights of the passengers to seats in the lifeboats, one might argue that these rights entailed duties of the shipowners to see to it that before the ship left port it was suitably equipped with state of the art life-saving equipment, and that their failure to provide adequate lifeboats violated their passenger's rights. Unless, of course, there is reason to think—as surely there was—that the passengers in effect waived their rights to such safety measures, or tacitly consented to the lack thereof, because they knew full well the risk they were taking if the ship were to sink, and they chose to run this risk because they couldn't afford transoceanic passage on a ship more adequately outfitted.

X

More light is shed on the Holmes case if we look briefly at how Holmes's conduct might be judged under subsequent law. Critical to that is one final principle, *Choose the Lesser Evil.* This principle is familiar to lawyers as the one that governs cases in which, as here, there is a choice only between evils. For example, the Model Penal Code endorses the principle of Choose the Lesser Evil, and cites examples to illustrate the principle in action: "An ambulance may pass a traffic light. Mountain climbers lost in a storm may take refuge in a house or may appropriate provisions. Cargo may be jettisoned . . . to preserve the vessel. . . . A druggist may dispense a drug without the requisite prescription to alleviate grave distress in an emergency." In all such cases, the unlawful and harmful conduct is legally justified. It will be noticed, however, that all these examples are quite remote from conduct causing the death of an innocent person in order to save the lives of other innocents—the conduct of which Holmes was found guilty.

Lest you think that the choice of evils doctrine as presented in the Model Penal Code is of recent or peculiarly American development, unavailable to courts of the previous century, consider some remarks made a century ago by Sir James Fitzjames Stephen, an influential Victorian jurist and theorist on issues of law and morals. He cites "the choice of evils" as a justifiable ground for violating the law, and offers as an example of the application of this doctrine a case precisely in point, in which "A boat being too full of passengers to float, some are thrown overboard." Sir James would have instructed Holmes's jury to acquit, provided they accepted the defense's view of the facts.

However, a contrary voice heard midway in time between Judge Stephen and the Model Penal Code, that of the distinguished American jurist Benjamin N. Cardozo, deserves attention. Commenting on the Holmes case, Cardozo observed:

> Where two or more are overtaken by a common disaster, there is no right on the part of one to save the lives of some by killing another. There is no rule of human jettison. Men there will often be who, when told that their going will be the salvation of the remnant, will choose the nobler part and make the plunge into the waters. In that supreme moment the darkness for them will be illumined by the thought that those behind will ride to safety. If none of such mold are found aboard the boat, or too few to save the others, the human freight must be left to meet the chances of the waters. Who shall choose in such an hour between the victims and the saved? Who shall know when masts and sails of rescue may emerge out of the fog?

Justice Cardozo would have voted to convict Holmes, and whether he would have allowed any defense of superior orders, of necessity, or of choice of the lesser evil in homicide cases seems doubtful. The extreme caution of Justice Cardozo's counsel, however, is not the prevailing one, as the Model Penal Code's treatment of the same problem shows. In its commentary on the passage quoted above, the Code says this:

> It would be particularly unfortunate to exclude homicidal conduct from the scope of the defense [of choice of evils]. . . . [C]onduct that results in taking life may promote the very value sought to be protected by the law of homicide. . . . The life of every individual must be taken . . . to be of equal value and the numerical preponderance in the lives saved compared to those sacrificed surely should establish legal justification for the act. . . . Although the view is not universally held that it is ethically preferable to take one innocent life than to have many lives lost, most persons probably think a net saving of lives is ethically warranted if the choice

among lives to be saved is not unfair. Certainly the law should permit such a choice.

How does all this bear on what the law would say today about Holmes's conduct? I remind you that his counsel at trial did not offer a choice of evils defense, the prosecution did not introduce mention of such a defense in order to criticize it, and the trial judge did not instruct the jury either way on this defense. This line of argument thus played no explicit role in the proceedings against Holmes at all—although one could argue that it was buried in the controversy at trial over whether any of the deaths was really "necessary."

But supposing it had been explicitly introduced by the defense—what then? Under the criteria afforded by the Model Penal Code, Holmes should have been acquitted—except, some might reply, for the clause in the commentary on the Code imposing the requirement that "the choice among lives to be saved is not unfair." We have seen that it was essential to the court's reasoning that Holmes unfairly chose those to be sacrificed, first in exempting all the crew, and second in not choosing by a fair lottery those to be sacrificed. So, on closer look, it appears that under the Code Holmes might well have been convicted, as he was, although not quite for the reasons that Justice Cardozo implied he should have been.

However, I have previously argued that these two points—Holmes's failure to put any of the crew in the lifeboat at risk, and his failure to choose a fair system of sacrifice—on which the court seems to rest so much weight are not so conclusive against Holmes as the court seemed to think. (I note in passing that Judge Stephen, in a brief comment on the Holmes case, declared that the rationale resulting in the instructions to the jury was "over refined"—just what one might expect from a card-carrying utilitarian such as he.) Indeed, once you grant that the choice of evils defense is legitimate in some cases, it will be difficult to refuse to apply it also in some cases of homicide. And once that is done, it will be extremely difficult to refuse to favor acquittal for Holmes. Of course, Holmes's actions represent the acting out of a terrible choice—a point blurred by any principle, theory, or reasoning that would too easily justify Holmes. But he is not to be faulted for trying to reduce the scope of the tragedy, any more than he is to be faulted for bringing about the circumstances in which a dreadful choice had to be made.

It will not have gone entirely unnoticed that the Model Penal Code appears to rest its support for the principle Choose the Lesser Evil on the weak fact—although it is a fact—that "most persons probably think a net saving of lives is ethically warranted if the choice among lives to be saved is not unfair." Can we say no more on behalf of this principle than that "most people probably think" it is sound? Philosophers are tempted to solve this kind of problem by taking refuge in some more abstract and inclusive principle from which a derivative principle, such as Choose the Lesser Evil, can be deduced. That is not the path I will take here. For principles such as this one are no better than the results they dictate in application, and we have no independent standpoint from which to render any final assessment of those results apart from prior or concurrent adoption of the very principles we would test. The U.S. Supreme Court once remarked that the Constitution is not a "suicide pact." Well, neither is morality. It is also not a conspiracy of assassins. Surely, the role of a moral code or of moral principles is to constrain our choices in order to preserve our values, chief among which is equal respect for persons and for their lives, autonomy, and welfare. One way to do that in the circumstances in which Seaman Holmes found himself was to do just what he did.

XI

As I mentioned earlier, the prosecution prevailed; the judge virtually instructed the jury to bring in a verdict against Holmes of guilty of manslaughter as charged, and it did. However, noting that Holmes had already been in jail for several months and that there were many (in the words of the court reporter) "circumstances in the affair" (by which he meant what we would call mitigating factors), Judge Baldwin sentenced Holmes to six months of solitary confinement at hard labor and a fine of $20. Although pardon was sought from President Zachary Taylor, it was denied. Thus was the majesty of the law and respect for human life upheld on the high seas, even in tragic circumstances.

In the end, I think Holmes had grounds for complaint at the way he was served. There is no reason to believe that he alone was guilty, if any were guilty, of manslaughter. There is no reason to believe that his interpretation of the first mate's orders, which had him acting on the principle of Save Families Plus Crew, was inappropriate; the record fails to show that the mate or any of the crew objected to acting on this principle as or after Holmes took the initiative to act on it. (The record does show that some passengers objected.) There is no reason for us to believe that he believed, or that he should have known, he was carrying out unlawful orders of his superior officer. Weight must surely be given to Holmes's good-faith belief that, in acting as he did, he was carrying out the lawful orders of his superior officer, orders duly weighed in the circumstances and for which that officer must eventually answer, if anyone must. The selection principle of Save Families Plus Crew, under which Holmes acted, has a claim to be at least as good in the circumstances as any feasible alternative principle. And one might even try to outflank the way the Kantian Condition vetoes this principle by arguing that in accepting voyage on the high seas the passengers tacitly consented to abide by the judgment of the ship's officers in fair weather and in foul, and so they have no complaint on Kantian grounds for the decision by the first mate to select all and only single male passengers to be sacrificed for the good of the rest.

True, all this taken together does not erase the fact that Holmes did assist in causing more than a dozen homicides. He did throw and help others throw overboard a number of persons in full knowledge that they would soon die by drowning, even though he did it without malice or other obviously blameworthy motive. The fact that Holmes stood to gain (although not he alone) from the deaths he caused cannot be denied; but as it is not clear he stood to gain unfairly, we must not let this weigh too heavily against him. In sum, I cannot conclude that Holmes did the wrong thing in acting as he did, and so I cannot think his punishment—lenient though it must have seemed in its day—was deserved.

PRINCIPLES AND GOALS

Save the Most Possible: Choose whatever selection principle the application of which requires the sacrifice of the fewest persons.

Passenger's Safety First: Choose whatever selection principle the application of which most effectively promotes the safety of all the passengers.

Save Families, Women, and Children: Sacrifice single men.

Save Families Plus Crew: Sacrifice single male passengers (= the operative selection principle).

First Reached, First Overboard: Sacrifice those most easily reached.

Save the Best: Protect from sacrifice all those most fit, according to some criterion of fitness.

Last In, First Out (or *Seniority*): Sacrifice those who entered the boat last (thus having overloaded it).

Self-sacrifice of the Weak: Let those who are weak, infirm, aged, or otherwise burdensome sacrifice themselves.

Sacrifice the Weak: Let those who are weak, infirm, aged, or otherwise burdensome be sacrificed.

Equal Risk: Sacrifice those chosen for that fate by means of a fair lottery.

Decimation: Out of a set of persons, a few of whom must die if the majority is to survive, sacrifice every *n*th person.

Sailor's Duty to Obey: Sailors are duty-bound to carry out, to the best of their ability, the reasonable orders of their superiors.

Sole Means Necessary to the End: If the deaths of a few are necessary to the surivival of the many, then those deaths are justified.

The Kantian Condition: No one has the right to use another person solely as a means to the former's ends without the latter's voluntary informed consent.

Shared Disaster: When most could survive if a few would sacrifice themselves, but no volunteers come forward, it is better if none survive.

Sailor's Duty of Self-sacrifice: If risk of death is to be run, it is the crew, not any of the passengers, who have the duty to take the risk.

Choose the Lesser Evil: Given a finite set of alternatives, each of which will cause harm to the innocent, choose the alternative that causes the least harm (or the least net harm, if some alternatives cause both benefit and harm).

Defense of Superior Orders: A subordinate is not at fault for carrying out the wrongful orders of his superior, provided he did not know and could not reasonably have been expected to know that the orders were wrongful.

TWO

The Speluncean Explorers and the Death of Roger Whetmore

I

The case of the speluncean explorers, which transpired in the 1940s, was one of the most troublesome criminal cases any jurisdiction could face. The words quoted below are those of Chief Justice Truepenny; they prefaced his opinion and those of his colleagues on the bench, which paved the way for their decision. In this opening portion of the Chief Justice's opinion he sets forth the facts of the case:

> The four defendants are members of the Speluncean Society, an organization of amateurs interested in the exploration of caves. Early in May [of last year] they, in company with Roger Whetmore, then also a member of the Society, entered into the interior of a limestone cavern of the type found in the Central Plateau of this Commonwealth. While they were in a position remote from the entrance to the cave, a landslide occurred. Heavy boulders fell in such a manner as to block completely the only known opening to the cave. When the

men discovered their predicament they settled themselves near the obstructed entrance to wait until a rescue party would remove the detritus that prevented them from leaving their underground prison. On the failure of Whetmore and the defendants to return to their homes, the Secretary of the Society was notified by their families. . . . A rescue party was promptly dispatched to the spot.

The task of rescue proved one of overwhelming difficulty. . . . The work of removing the obstruction was several times frustrated by fresh landslides. . . . Success was finally achieved on the thirty-second day after the men entered the cave.

Since it was known that the explorers had carried with them only scant provisions, and since it was also known that there was no animal or vegetable matter within the cave on which they might subsist, anxiety was early felt that they might meet death by starvation before access to them could be obtained. . . .

From the testimony of the defendants, which was accepted by the jury, it appears that it was Whetmore who first proposed that they might find the nutriment without which survival was impossible in the flesh of one of their own number. It was also Whetmore who first proposed the use of some method of casting lots, calling the attention of the defendants to a pair of dice he happened to have with him. The defendants were at first reluctant to adopt so desperate a procedure, but . . . they finally agreed on the plan proposed by Whetmore. . . .

Before the dice were cast, however, Whetmore declared he withdrew from the arrangement, as he had decided on reflection to wait another week before embracing an expedient so frightful and odious. The others charged him with a breach of faith and proceeded to cast the dice. When it came Whetmore's turn, the dice were cast for him by one of the defendants, and he was asked to declare any objections he might have to the

> fairness of the throw. He stated that he had no such objections. The throw went against him, and he was then put to death and eaten by his companions.
>
> After the rescue of the defendants . . . they were indicted for the murder of Roger Whetmore. . . . In a lengthy special verdict the jury found the facts as I have related them above, and found further that if on these facts the defendants were guilty of the crime charged against them, then they found the defendants guilty. On the basis of this verdict, the trial judge ruled that the defendants were guilty of murdering Roger Whetmore. The judge then sentenced them to be hanged, the law of our Commonwealth permitting him no discretion with respect to the penalty to be imposed. After the release of the jury, its members joined in a communication to the Chief Executive asking that the sentence be commuted to an imprisonment for six months. The trial judge addressed a similar communication to the Chief Executive. As yet no action with respect to these pleas has been taken, as the Chief Executive is apparently awaiting our disposition of this petition of error.

The issue before Chief Justice Truepenny's Supreme Court was whether to overturn or sustain the decision of the lower court that had found the four surviving spelunkers guilty of murder. On this crucial matter, as their differing written opinions show, there was very little agreement among the appellate judges. They concluded their deliberations with a deeply divided vote: Two of the five judges (although not for the same reasons) voted to sustain the lower court verdict, another two (although, again, not for the same reasons) voted to reverse it, and the fifth—declaring that he was "wholly unable to resolve the doubts that beset me about the law of this case"—announced his withdrawal. In this jurisdiction, as in others, a split vote on appeal amounts to an affirmance of the lower court's decision.

Lest the reader wonder any further who Truepenny is, what Supreme Court he presided over as Chief Justice, and exactly when and where these tragic events transpired, I should explain that the plight of the speluncean explorers is entirely hypothetical, as is the Supreme Court of Newgarth in which these fictional proceedings took place. Woven out of whole cloth for pedagogical purposes in the early 1940s by the late Lon Fuller (at the time professor of jurisprudence at Harvard Law School), the case was first published in 1949. In a postscript explaining his reasons for constructing the case, Fuller said that he invented it for "the sole purpose of bringing into a common focus certain divergent philosophies of law and government." Those "divergent philosophies" appear in the reasoning he contrived to put into the mouths of his five imaginary judges. Few if any hypothetical cases in the pedagogy of modern jurisprudence can rival this one in popularity; law students by the thousands have read and discussed it for nearly half a century. Whether the fictional spelunkers were ever fictionally executed, however, we do not know; Fuller carefully avoided carrying his fanciful narrative beyond the point of his Supreme Court's affirmance on appeal.

My purpose is not to review and evaluate what Fuller called the "divergent philosophies of law and government" he put on display in this case. Instead, I want to focus attention on the moral issues raised by the killing of Roger Whetmore and on the reasoning surrounding the outcome of the case and possible alternative outcomes. Whetmore and his unfortunate companions and their conduct in the cave present us with several moral questions, including one we have met before:

When not all can survive, who (if any) ought to die? Whereas Fuller wanted the reader of this case to reflect on the legal rationale underlying an appellate court judgment of acquittal or affirmance in order to set forth the best decision that the Supreme Court of Newgarth could make in this case, I am concerned with matters to which his five judges gave little or no attention. The central question for me is the propriety with which Whetmore is killed in the circumstances related in the narrative; that is, whether Whetmore's death can be justified, or at least excused, or neither.

II

We might start by considering the difference between trying to justify and trying to excuse the surviving spelunkers for killing Whetmore. For reasons not entirely clear, the distinction between justifying and excusing has been hopelessly confused in the two most famous real cases like the fictional case under discussion. One is the American case of *United States v. Holmes* (1842), examined in the previous chapter. In *Holmes,* defense attorney Armstrong said to the court on behalf of his client: "We contend . . . that what is honestly and reasonably believed to be certain death will justify self-defense to the degree requisite for excuse." Here, the learned counsellor implies that if enough of a justification can be given, it will qualify as an adequate excuse. The other is the English case of *Regina v. Dudley & Stephens* (1884), some forty years later. In this case the appellate judge, Lord Coleridge, compounded the confusion when he began his review of the case on appeal by observing: "Now it is admitted that the deliberate killing of this unoffending boy was clearly murder, unless the killing can be justified by some well-recognized excuse admitted by the law." Here the confusion is the other way around, as though one way to justify deliberately causing harm to the innocent is to excuse it.

Unlike these lawyers, I think it is possible, as well as desirable, to make a hard and fast distinction between justification and excuse. Neither is a species of the other, and in chapter 1 I distinguished between them as follows: One *justifies* causing harm to another by showing that one did it deliberately and after due reflection because in the circumstances that was the right (or the best) thing to do. One *excuses* someone from blame for the harm done to another by conceding that it was wrong to cause the harm, but that nevertheless in the circumstances it couldn't be helped and that therefore one can't really be blamed for it.

The distinction so formulated applies to the conduct of the speluncean explorers straightaway. If Whetmore's death is to be excused, then it must be because the surviving spelunkers killed him in ignorance, or out of an irresistible impulse, or by mistake, accident, or misadventure, or in some other way that relieves them of fault. But Whetmore's death was not caused in any of these ways; the killing of Whetmore by his companions surely could have been avoided—neither he nor anyone else had to be chosen to die. So there is no ground on which to contemplate excusing his killers for causing his death. Instead, their act must be justified—or at least morally permitted. If that is impossible, then killing him was wrong and unjustified.

The neat distinction I have invoked between excusing and justifying harm is often blurred in the law in the so-called defense of "necessity": The law sometimes treats necessity as an excuse and other times treats it as a justification. It seems to me clearer to say that if necessity is a defense—a strategy already explored in the previous chapter—then it is a defense that will *justify* deliberately causing harm to the innocent. Inattention, ignorance, helplessness, or any disability or incapacity typical of the excuses that negate otherwise faulty responsibility are all precluded by the rational judgment one exercises in acting to save oneself or others when faced with the necessity to do so.

III

A few paragraphs earlier, I quoted the defense attorney in the Holmes case as referring to death caused in "self-defense" as justified killing. That remark invites us to consider whether Whetmore's death could be justified on the ground that the surviving spelunkers killed him in self-defense. Self-defense is a well-established principle in both law and morality as a ground for justifiably harming—and even killing—another person. Few save absolute pacifists will challenge the legitimacy of the principle that one may kill others in self-defense when one's own life is put in jeopardy by another through no fault of one's own. Surely we must agree that the lives of the five spelunkers were at risk; they clearly believed this, and it was reasonable for them to believe it. I think we can also agree that killing in self-defense is within one's rights—although adequately framing the constraints on justified killing in self-defense provides a convincing demonstration that it is not easy to state a moral principle with sufficient precision so that it is free of unwanted consequences and endless qualifications.

Setting that problem to one side, the killing of Whetmore

by the other spelunkers was clearly *not* a deed carried out in self-defense. One cannot kill or wound in self-defense except in response to some aggressive lethal act or attempt at such an act by another person. But no one alleged that Whetmore committed, or attempted to commit, or even threatened to commit any aggression against anyone in the cave. As a result, the issue of self-defense in this case is merely a red herring.

On the other hand, it is true that the four spelunkers killed Whetmore in an attempt to secure their self-preservation. They believed that only by an act of cannibalism on their part could any survive. They probably also believed that expediency, as well as common decency, required them to kill before they ate, and that Whetmore was the person properly chosen for them to feed on. Self-defense is, of course, one form that self-protection can take; quite possibly, what leads some to introduce considerations of self-defense in the conduct of those who killed Whetmore is a simple confusion between the genus (self-preservation) and one of its species (self-defense). So, what we need to examine is the idea or goal of self-preservation.

IV

Even if it is granted that the surviving spelunkers did not kill Whetmore in their own self-defense, some may want to argue that the killing represents more than the acting out of a desire by the spelunkers for their self-preservation. After all, this argument would run, their very right to life was at stake—not, to be sure, as a result of Whetmore's aggression, but as a result of their collective misfortune—and thus their right of self-preservation comes into play. In the circumstances of their imprisonment in the cave, that right entitled them to take Whetmore's life. After all, if they had a right to live, as they did, then they also must have a right to choose a means sufficient to that end, which they did in the form of the lottery. So the death of Whetmore is justified by the right to life of the other spelunkers.

I do not dispute that the spelunkers had a right to life; each of us surely has such a right, although formulating that right correctly is no small task. Given such a right, it is tempting to insist that the spelunkers also had a right to some means sufficient to that end. To say this is to rely on what might be called the *Rights Principle,* to the effect that one who has a right to an end has a right to some means sufficient to that end. (As an aside, notice that this principle is quite distinct from the point Kant made when he said that whoever wills the end wills some means to that end. Willing a means to an end is entirely different from having a right to pursue some means to an end, for I can will to do something I have no right to do.)

Unfortunately or not, as the case may be, the Rights principle is treacherous. Although it is true that the spelunkers's right to life together with the Rights principle would give the spelunkers the right to kill Whetmore as the means to their end, we cannot accept the conclusion that they had a right to kill him. After all, isn't it obvious that Whetmore, too, had a right to life, a right every bit as robust as those of his four companions? Well, if that is true, then they had to choose a means to their end that did not trespass against his rights. Not only that, they also had to consider the possibility that there might not be *any* means on which they could rightly act to protect their own lives. Leaving that troublesome possibility to one side, the means the other spelunkers chose was not consistent with respecting Whetmore's rights. To see why, let us explore what is wrong with the argument waiting to be invoked to show that the four surviving spelunkers were, after all, justified in the means they chose.

The argument for such justification asserts that because Whetmore consented indirectly to his own death, and because one cannot protest as unjust to oneself whatever one has willingly authorized others to do, Whetmore's death was justified. The major premise of this argument—the principle that one cannot wrong oneself by a voluntary act of one's own—we may call *Hobbes's Principle,* because Thomas Hobbes made it a prominent feature of his conception of political sovereignty. (The Hobbesian sovereign can do no wrong to his subjects because whatever he does, he does with their tacit consent. In his official capacity, he always acts with the authority the subjects have conferred on him, for he is in effect their agent and so may use his judgment as he sees fit.) Whether or not Hobbes's principle is sound, it entails, as a matter of conceptual necessity, that I cannot violate my own rights, or make myself a victim of injustice. In short, I cannot voluntarily wrong myself. Harm myself I can, of course, do; a typical result of one's rash or imprudent actions is harm to self or at least unreasonable risk of such harm. But such harms to self are not self-inflicted injustices, or violations of one's own rights. (This reasoning may not be immune to criticism, but I do not propose to challenge it here.)

V

The issue that needs closer examination is the minor premise in the argument, that Whetmore indirectly consented to his own death. Of course, he did not *directly* consent to die, as it might be said Captain Oates did during Scott's ill-fated attempt to reach the South Pole in 1910. As we noted in chapter 1, Oates acted as a self-appointed martyr, offering his life to serve the needs of his companions. Yet Whetmore, it will be said, indirectly consented to his own death when he directly consented to join the others in a fair selection procedure that he knew gave him one chance in five of being the one chosen to die for the sake of the others. That scheme and his consent to it, plus the outcome of a fair throw of the dice for Whetmore, made him the odd man out. Whatever a court of law might say about killing a person under such circumstances, morality cannot so easily judge the killing to be wrong. Indeed, we can say more: If Whetmore solemnly consented to a procedure that—when fairly applied—results in his death, a procedure he knew in advance was being used as a lethal selection procedure, then his consent imposes on him the obligation to let the others kill him, just as it gives to the others the right to do so.

Some have thought—John Locke, notably, among them—that no one has the right to dispose of his or her life, because each of us is alive at all thanks to God's will; we remain in permanent debt for this greatest of all gifts, our very lives. On this view, what Whetmore did was indirectly, suicide (or, as Hamlet more vividly put it, "self-slaughter"), and what the four surviving spelunkers did to him was outright murder. In the language of rights, we may waive our right to life, as Captain Oates did; and we may forfeit this right, as every murderer does (so Locke said); but we cannot alienate it—give, sell, or transfer it to another. Locke in effect holds that we suffer from a certain disability, or lack of power, namely, the disability to take our own lives. We cannot give to another the power of life and death over us, because we have no such power to give.

A modern secular theory of rights would not endorse such a conclusion, however. For no secular theory of rights could grant the initial premise—that we have what natural or human rights we possess because we are creatures of God's will and our lives a divine gift. Rather, a secular theory of rights would surely show, among other things, that each of us has a right to die under conditions and at a time and place of our own choosing, insofar as such choice is feasible and violates no other person's rights. This is not the place to argue the matter further, so I will put both the Lockean theory of rights and reflections on an alternative theory to the side without further discussion.

VI

Some will object to all the reasoning so far on the ground that it is irrelevant, since it flies in the face of the fact that Whetmore withdrew from the lottery before the dice were thrown, and that unless it can be shown that his withdrawal was illegitimate or somehow null and void, it cannot be argued that he indirectly consented to his own death. On the contrary, so this objection goes, the narrative of the case makes it plain that he explicitly withdrew his prior consent. And this leaves Whetmore in a position comparable to that of the young cabin boy in what became one of the most notorious criminal cases of the nineteenth century, *Regina v. Dudley & Stephens*: the boy, adrift on the high seas in a lifeboat with two adult sailors, was murdered without any pretense of having his consent by his companions in order to cannibalize him.

Forceful though this reasoning is, others will reply that its conclusion cannot be true because (as the narrative also clearly states) when Whetmore was asked whether he had "any objections to the fairness of the throw"—the throw of the dice on his behalf by one of his fellow spelunkers—he stated "he had no such objections." What ground for an objection could he have had? Might he have thought the dice were loaded against him? (They were his dice!) Or that the dice-thrower carefully caromed the dice so their roll would result in Whetmore's losing? These and similar objections to the fairness of the throw have no plausible basis in the assumed facts; so, in the absence of some such objections, Whetmore could hardly complain that the throw itself was unfair.

So far, so good. But Whetmore's failure to protest the fairness *of* the throw does not entail his concession that it was fair to throw *for* him in the first place, and so does not entail that he was bound by the outcome of the throw and the rest given the right to kill him. Compare Shirley Jackson's famous gothic short story "The Lottery"; the last words uttered by the girl chosen to be stoned to death are "It isn't fair, it isn't right"—but whether she is protesting the practice of her village's annual stoning by lottery or protesting the fairness of the lottery through which she was selected remains unclear (just as it is unclear why Whetmore did not protest a throw being made for him when he had already announced his withdrawal from the lottery). I think Whetmore must have thought it was *unfair* to throw for him, since he had declared his withdrawal from the lottery before the throw. Far from conceding the fairness of including himself in the lottery, his refusal to contest the fairness of the throw amounted at most to silent acquiescence in whatever the decision and action of his companions would be. Accordingly, I think it wrong to argue that Whetmore's death was justified by his own indirect consent. On the contrary, he had expressly withdrawn his consent to participating in the lethal lottery procedure and thus to being morally bound by its outcome. And if this is true, then it is also true that the killing of Whetmore was done without any moral authority, and the Rights principle is illegitimate. (In passing, one might wonder whether the other spelunkers would have been so insistent on ignoring his declared withdrawal if the throw had gone not against him but against one of them.)

VII

For either of two reasons, some will balk at this conclusion—just as the other spelunkers did, when they charged Whetmore with acting in "bad faith" in trying to withdraw. The first and more obvious reason for balking is that no one's participation in the lottery was unilaterally revocable. On this view, nothing Whetmore could say or do after the initial agreement to hold a survival lottery could exempt him from participation. He needed the permission of his fellow spelunkers to withdraw, and they didn't give it. It is as if they were standing here on what we might call a principle of *Irrevocability*: One may not withdraw from a solemn agreement without the consent of the other part(ies) to that agreement.

Such a view of the matter and this principle of Irrevocability will not withstand scrutiny, however. If Whetmore's words of consent to participate were sufficient to involve him in the lottery in the first place, as they clearly were, then his subsequent words of withdrawal ought to be sufficient to that end, too—unless, of course, there were intervening events that altered the circumstances of the other lottery participants in relevant ways.

For example, suppose you and I agree on a certain cooperative undertaking, and in anticipation thereof you invest time and money that you otherwise would not have. I abruptly announce I'm withdrawing from the deal, but you refuse permission, arguing that you suddenly face loss of your entire investment. Surely, whatever the law of contract may say, morality declares that I am *not* free to withdraw without further ado. Your legitimate expectation of benefit created by our agreement, plus your action on that expectation and its cost to you, alters the situation in relevant ways. At the least, if I withdraw I owe you some compensation, since without my initial agreement you would not have incurred the costs in question.

In the case of the spelunkers, however, Whetmore proposed to withdraw before the throw, and no other events of the requisite sort had transpired between his proposal of the lottery and his declared withdrawal. Whetmore, as the lawyers might say, had received no "consideration"—he had not gained anything in advance of his performance—from the other spelunkers arising out of their mutual agreement. Nor had they incurred any costs. The only block to his right to withdraw from the lottery thus disappears. He did not need the permission of the others to withdraw; his timely say-so was enough. (We need not decide what we should make of Whetmore's situation had he sought to withdraw only *after* he learned he had lost in the lottery.)

Before leaving this line of argument, we need to consider another form of this complaint against Whetmore by the other spelunkers. Suppose they argue that, by his withdrawal, Whetmore has increased the likelihood that one of the remaining spelunkers will turn out to be the unlucky one to be sacrified. To be precise, the likelihood that any one of the five spelunkers will lose is 20 percent (one chance in five); if they respect Whetmore's withdrawal and still want to conduct a lottery, the chances that any one of the four remaining spelunkers will lose increases to 25 percent (one chance in four). But, they add, he has no right to raise the probabilities against them in this way by shifting the entire burden of risk onto their shoulders. True, a 5 percent increase in probability is a small increase, and it may not satisfy the lawyer's idea of contractual consideration. But, his friends in the cave might argue, surely morality ought to be able to get a grip on the relevance of this increase. What could Whetmore say in reply?

Well, he ought to concede that his withdrawal does increase the risk of death for each of the other four by 5 percent if they want to go ahead with a lottery among themselves; and to that extent their objection is correct. But his principal reply ought to be that their criticism completely begs the question, because it assumes that there will be or ought to be a lethal lottery in the first place, when in fact there is no moral necessity for such a lottery at all. To be sure, it was he who proposed the idea of the lottery, but it is the rest of the spelunkers who now insist on it (as well as on his participation). That is merely their preference, not a matter of necessity or of any right they have over his conduct. Thus, he is free to act on his preference to join them or to withdraw.

A second line of reasoning against Whetmore's withdrawal takes us in a very different direction. The argument here ignores the issue of quasi-contractual obligations and stresses instead that if Whetmore withdraws, or is allowed to withdraw, then his act is disloyal to his comrades in the cave. After all, the five of them tacitly agreed to take the risks of their adventure together; they were bound not by legalistic chains but by fibers of morality. *Share and Share Alike* perhaps expresses this in familiar language—a principle that makes it unacceptable for Whetmore unilaterally to refuse to share any further. He cannot have the last word in this manner; he ought not to be allowed to withdraw.

What is interesting about this objection is that it ignores the vocabulary, as well as the principles, of rights and obligations, and invokes instead a picture of a tiny intentional community suddenly faced with the terrors and risks of being buried alive and of bonds of loyalty that may not be severed. But how persuasive and conclusive is this picture? After all, it is not as if Whetmore's desire to withdraw gave him, or was intended to give him, some advantage at the expense of others. Instead, his withdrawal was a self-inspired virtual death sentence, since the others who survive the lottery are not likely to invite him to join in their meal and he surely has no claim to do so. What complaint, really, do his four comrades have against him for not being one of the boys, ready as they are to risk all on the throw of the dice? Invoking the demands of *Loyalty to the Group* as the principle that shows anyone's withdrawal from the lottery is wrong and impermissible is merely another way of ignoring individual rights.

VIII

It is now time to return to the issue of necessity raised earlier, because it gives rise to a completely different line of argument in defense of killing Whetmore—an argument that rests more or less on consequentialist utilitarian grounds. Thus, it is an argument with three important features: First, it in effect redefines the death of Whetmore simply as a killing, rejecting as overblown the description of his death as murder; second, it settles the morality of that killing by reference to its consequences for all concerned; third, it relies on collecting or aggregating the benefits and losses resulting from that act. On this argument, one starts with the premise that where human life and death are concerned, it is always better for some to live than none, and better for more rather than fewer to survive. This is the goal I had occasion to identify in the previous chapter and called there Save the Most Possible. To this we may add the premise that where it is necessary that some die for many others to live, the deaths of the former are justified. This is a principle also identified in the previous chapter, there called the Sole Means Necessary to the End principle. After all, human life in itself is a good thing, and so the more human lives saved, the better. Thus, on this reasoning, Whetmore is killed so that four others may live; the only alternative anyone can see to having at least one die is for all to die. Since that alternative is less preferable under the principles above, the four spelunkers are justified in killing Whetmore. After all, four alive and one dead is better than five dead.

But now consider this parallel hypothetical case, a version of what is known in the literature of applied ethics as Transplant. Suppose I said to you:

> I'm an organ transplant surgeon, and I have several patients who are dying—although each could survive if suitable trans-

> plants were made. Two of my patients need a kidney each, another needs a liver, a fourth needs a heart, and the fifth needs a complete blood transfusion. Your doctor has informed me that you are dying of an inoperable brain tumor, and my assistants have discovered that your blood and tissue type are perfect for transplants to my patients. So, rather than wait for your natural death, by which time all of my patients will be dead, I propose to carve you up immediately to save them. After all, where human life is concerned, you surely agree that where not all can live, it is better that some live, and so you must agree that it is much better for four to live and one to die rather than for all five to die.

Mindful of the discussion of the Whetmore case so far, you might object to being the sacrificial organ donor. First, you might object that you have no reason to believe that you were chosen to sacrifice your life by a fair procedure. Why were you, among all the other possible donors, selected? This objection has some force, but not much. For suppose it turns out that you are the only suitable donor on medical grounds; or, although you are only one of many medically suitable donors, you are alone among them in facing an untimely death in the near future. Where saving life is necessary and the costs of doing so can be borne in fact by only one, or borne best by only one, then that person will have to bear them—or so the utilitarian will argue.

Fortunately, you have another objection that is much stronger. No matter how you were selected, you will insist that you have no obligation or duty to sacrifice yourself for these others, and so the surgeon has no right to carve you up, because you never consented, directly or indirectly, to any procedure that would have you die to save these others. The trouble with the utilitarian argument is that it either assumes without warrant your tacit consent to the sacrifice, or it ignores without warrant the relevance of your failure or refusal to give consent. And so, as we saw earlier, because Whetmore gave no such consent, his death can be justified by the argument we are exploring only by flouting his rights. Of course, it would be generous beyond belief for you to cut short your life for the sake of the transplant surgeon's patients—utter strangers to you—who will die without prompt organ transplants, just as it would be generous for Whetmore to offer himself as a sacrifice to the welfare of his companions. Whetmore could have been a hero for his companions, and you for those five patients, as Captain Oates was for his fellow explorers. But no one has the right to *take* Whetmore's—or your—life to achieve these beneficial results just because some such action is "necessary" to save other's lives. We see here, as in the Holmes case discussed in the previous chapter, that what I there called the Kantian Condition blocks reliance on the Sole Means Necessary to the End principle. The Kantian Condition forbids one from using another solely as the means to one's own ends, thus raising a barrier to treating the worth of others and their ends as less worthy than oneself and one's own ends—even in cases in which there is no other means to the end.

Before moving on, we might ask whether Whetmore ought nevertheless to go along with the outcome of the lottery. On what ground might we argue that he ought to do so? Not that he has an obligation or duty to do so, and not that the others have a right to demand that he do so; those arguments have been seen to fail. And also not because the others want him to do so: We cannot derive what Whetmore ought to do from what others want him to do. What, then, about the fact that it would be a good thing for the others if he did? Well, it would be a very good thing indeed for the others if Whetmore sacrificed himself for them. But we can't argue in general that because something would be a good thing for others if Jones did it, therefore Jones ought to do it. There are just too many good things each of us could do for others for it to be the case that the goodness-for-others of a thing is a sufficient reason one ought to do it. After all, an action's being a good thing for others does not distinguish it as preferable to other equally good (or even better) possible actions.

Can we get around this by arguing that the best thing Whetmore could do would be to sacrifice himself, and Whetmore, like everyone else, always ought to do whatever is the best thing? Let's grant the premise that we always ought to do whatever is the best thing for us to do, and infer that therefore Whetmore ought to do whatever is the best thing for him to do. But whether sacrificing his life *is* the best thing for him to do depends in part on whether that's what *he* wants to do, and on his *reasons* for wanting to do it. Saying flat out that it would be best if Whetmore sacrificed himself for the others and that he therefore ought to do it overlooks the fact that it would be good for Whetmore and three of the other spelunkers if the fourth among the others sacrificed himself, a sacrifice no better and no worse, no greater and no less, than Whetmore's would be. So this argument also fails to vindicate the killing of Whetmore, just as it fails to vindicate the killing of any other one of the spelunkers.

IX

What is at stake here can be expressed by means of a widely recognized moral principle: No innocent person's life shall be sacrificed (that is, taken without consent) simply to serve the needs of others—not even a majority of others. This principle—we might call it the *Right to Life* principle—is obviously just another way to state what I earlier called the Kantian Condition, which forbids using one person solely as a means to the ends of others. This is the principle that the surviving spelunkers violated, and it is the principle that would be violated if one were to act on the utilitarian reasons outlined above in the Transplant case—just as it would be violated by anyone who argues that because Whetmore's (or someone's) death in the cave is really "necessary," others may kill him (or someone) as they deem appropriate, no doubt using only some fair means of selection, such as a lottery, in order to advance their own prospects. Further, it is a principle incompatible with the Sole Means Necessary to the End principle, which holds that doing whatever is necessary to save the lives of others, and especially a large majority of others, is morally justified.

Some might ask why we should have so much confidence in the principle that no innocent person's life may be sacrificed simply to advance the welfare of others. Why should this Right to Life principle be preferred to other principles that lead to a different conclusion in this case? It does not seem sufficient to say that the principle protects inherently individual interests as no competing principle does—although I believe this to be true. For then we must ask why protecting such interests of one individual at the cost of many lives is so important. Nor is it enough to say that the Right to Life principle expresses a deeply rooted intuition shared by many of the most thoughtful moralists and moral theorists in our culture—although that is also true. In addition, it is also not enough to say that this principle, taken in conjunction with other moral principles similarly rooted in intuition, rounds out with greater consistency our entire set of moral principles than if we reject this principle in favor of some alternative—although I believe that this, too, is true.

Exactly what sort of argument that is not an argument along the lines sketched above would suffice here to pacify the skeptical is unclear to me. Yet I am quite discontent simply to declare a naked preference for this principle. In the end I am, I suppose, tacitly inviting the reader to share with me a certain vision of human life and of death with dignity (if I may use that much-abused phrase)—a vision in which moral agents respect one another in ways that require them to act on the Right to Life principle as I have stated it, rather than on any principle incompatible with it.

X

Can we at last, mindful of the foregoing discussion, state with any confidence what morality dictates, or advises, that the five spelunkers should have done in their cave? One moderately attractive proposal that is likely to have occurred to many goes as follows: First, Whetmore's comrades were bound to respect his withdrawal from the lethal lottery. They had no right to throw for him, or at least no right to act on that throw when it went against him. Second, it is nevertheless true that Whetmore's proposal of a lethal lottery was a sensible idea in the circumstances, and this is entirely independent of whether he ultimately chooses to be party to the lottery. If some must die for any to live, then those who are prepared to act on this consideration must select the sacrificial person(s) by a fair and feasible procedure. In the circumstances, only a lottery (invoking the principle of Equal Risk) satisfies this requirement—a point at which the case before us deviates sharply from the Holmes case discussed in the previous chapter. Third, with Whetmore's withdrawal behind them and the appropriateness of a lottery agreed upon by the others, the others should propose to conduct a lottery among themselves. They should agree that the lucky three would kill in order to cannibalize the unlucky fourth. Finally, they must make it clear to Whetmore that he will not be permitted to receive any nourishment from the body of the person chosen to be sacrificed. Whetmore has no right to profit from the sacrifice of others when he exempted himself from running any risk of being sacrificed himself. Given the situation, this would probably have led to Whetmore's death prior to rescue—but he could have no legitimate complaint against anyone for such an outcome.

This line of reasoning seems to rely on the proposition that the best thing to do in the circumstances is for at least some to live, provided they do so without being unfair to anyone else. But is this true? Does survival at any cost—or at what some would regard, perhaps, as any fair and reasonable cost—have such a great value? There seem to be but two possible situations to consider, as we have realized all along: Either all die or some die, and in the latter case it is only a question of who and how many and how they are to be selected. How could it be better for all to die rather than only some? It seems it cannot, at least as an abstract proposition. As at a comparable place in the previous chapter, here we find ourselves staring at the default position I there called Shared Disaster: the proposition that where some could survive only if others would volunteer to sacrifice themselves, but none will, then it is better if all die. Not an attractive outcome.

But now consider. Suppose I am one of the spelunkers; I wish to live as much as anyone, but I am frankly repelled by the idea of killing any of my comrades in order to eat his flesh and drink his blood—just as I am terrified at the thought of being killed by the others so that they can eat me. I can't summon the courage to offer myself as a sacrifice, and I can't overcome my scruples at the idea of participating in a lottery to decide whether my body is to be eaten by others or whether one of them is to be eaten by me. All versions of choosing to cause a death in the cave are repulsive to me. As for my eating another's body or being eaten by others—or even watching others feed on the corpse of our friend—it fills me with horror and disgust. Thus, bit by bit, I persuade myself that in this wretched cave, with no hope of help from the outside, it is better for me to die of dehydration and starvation than either to try to live by cannibalism or to die so that my body can feed others. (I leave to one side whether, were I to be the first to die from natural causes, I would then have any objection to my companion's seizing the opportunity to cannibalize my corpse, as happened among the survivors of a plane crash in the Andes in 1972, reported by Piers Paul Read in his book *Alive*.)

Suppose further that each of the spelunkers reasons in this way. Each believes that it is better for him to die a natural death than to live by killing and cannibalism or to be killed for later cannibalism by the others. Can we say that if the spelunkers were to reason in this way, they would have reached the wrong conclusion—that they would be in error about what the best thing is for them to do? After all, they cannot expect to live forever—no one can—and the unsought and undesired circumstances of their demise in the cave still leaves them with more choice than many others have of how and when they are to die.

XI

What we are now considering is whether it is really true that where not all can survive, it is better that some survive, given what may turn out to be necessary for any to do so. I think it is doubtful at best, since the proposition in question as it stands fails to take into account any other preferences or considerations of those whose survival is at issue. Where none of the spelunkers wants to be killed or to kill, we might imagine one of them articulating the argument for all of them as follows:

> Yes, it's all very well to say that where not all can survive, it is better if some do and best if most do. Considered abstractly, we can all see the absurdity of Shared Disaster. But this just fails to take into account what may be required to avoid that outcome. In our situation, what it takes is being willing to kill and eat the flesh of another or being willing to be killed for that purpose. As it turns out, each of us here in the cave shrinks from that. We refuse to save ourselves by homicide and cannibalism. We refuse to invite or encourage any of us to offer himself as a sacrifice to the rest. What's best for us to do is to act so that we respect our considered judgment, even though that will certainly result in an untimely and perhaps unnecessary death for all of us.

I do not see why this argument is unreasonable or fatally flawed. It is simply extending to the general case the argument, or something very like it, that Whetmore probably used to convince himself to opt out of the lottery. Just as I think the other spelunkers must respect his decision to withdraw, I think we must respect all persons who decide to be (in Albert Camus's telling phrase) neither victims nor executioners. And that means we cannot accept survival as the paramount or dominant value, such that there *must* be some permissible means sufficient to achieve it under even the most extreme conditions. So I say that five who die trapped in the cave, rather than arrange for four to feast on one, live and die with greater dignity than four who kill a fifth without his consent in order to feast on him. Nowhere is it written that it is necessary for some to survive no matter what the cost to others. And as for the case in which the fifth consents to be killed and the other four agree to kill him in order to survive by eating his body, I can only say for myself that I would choose—or, acknowledging human frailty, hope I would choose—not to play either role.

PRINCIPLES AND GOALS

Self-defense: Causing harm (including death) to another is justified if doing so is a necessary condition of preventing one's victimization by the other's unprovoked and undeserved aggression.

Self-preservation: Causing harm (including death) to another is justified if doing so is a necessary condition of one's own survival.

The Rights Principle: One who has a right to the end has a right to some means sufficient to that end.

Hobbes's Principle: One cannot wrong oneself by any voluntary act of one's own.

Irrevocability: No one may withdraw from a solemn agreement without consent of the other part(ies).

Share and Share Alike: When some benefit or burden is to be distributed among several persons, each ought to have the same portion.

Loyalty to the Group: The needs of the group of which one is a member are to be placed ahead of any personal needs, interests, or rights.

The Utilitarian Principle: Among alternative acts open to the agent, choose whatever act offers the prospect of the greatest net balance of good over evil.

Save the Most Possible: Choose whatever course of action involves sacrificing as few persons as possible in order to save as many as possible.

Sole Means Necessary to the End: If the deaths of a few are necessary to the survival of the many, then those deaths are justified.

The Kantian Condition: No one has the right to use another person solely as a means to the former's ends without the latter's voluntary informed consent.

Right to Life: No innocent person's life may be sacrificed without consent to serve the needs of others. (Implied by the Kantian condition.)

Equal Risk: Sacrifice those chosen for that fate by means of a fair lottery.

Shared Disaster: When most could survive if a few would volunteer to sacrifice themselves, but no volunteers come forward, it is better if none survive.

THREE

Jim and the Indians in the Jungle Clearing

I

The scene of the dramatic events on which the ensuing discussion is focussed is as follows:

> Jim finds himself in the central square of a small South American town. Tied up against the wall are a row of twenty Indians, most terrified, a few defiant, in front of them several armed men in uniform. A heavy man in a sweat-stained khaki shirt turns out to be the captain in charge and, after a good deal of questioning of Jim which establishes that he got there by accident while on a botanical expedition, explains that the Indians are a random group of the inhabitants who, after recent acts of protest against the government, are just about to be killed to remind other possible protestors of the advantages of not protesting. However, since Jim is an honoured visitor from another land, the captain is happy to offer him a guest's privilege of killing one of the Indians himself. If Jim accepts, then as a special mark of the occasion, the other Indians will be let off. Of course, if Jim refuses, then there is no special occa-

> sion, and Pedro [the captain's subordinate] will do what he was about to do when Jim arrived, and kill them all. Jim, with some desperate recollection of schoolboy fiction, wonders whether if he got hold of a gun, he could hold the captain, Pedro, and the rest of the soldiers to threat, but it is quite clear from the setup that nothing of that kind is going to work: any attempt at that sort of thing will mean that all the Indians will be killed, and himself. The men against the wall, and the other villagers, understand the situation, and are obviously begging him to accept. What should he do?

Jim's predicament, you will be relieved to learn, is entirely hypothetical, just as was the plight of Roger Whetmore and his fellow spelunkers discussed in chapter 2. We owe this case to Bernard Williams, professor of philosophy at Oxford and at the University of California at Berkeley, who invented it some years ago and published it in *Utilitarianism For and Against,* a book he coauthored with his fellow-philosopher, J. J. C. Smart. Smart was For; Williams was Against, and he offered the story of Jim and the Indians in order to expose some important deficiencies in the moral theory of utilitarianism. I am also not friendly to utilitarianism, as the two previous chapters suggest; but I don't intend to use my discussion of this case as a stick with which to beat advocates of the principle of utility. Instead, I want to help Jim decide what to do, however that may be affected by utilitarian considerations.

Before we proceed, notice that—unlike the survivors in the longboat of the *William Brown,* and the speluncean explorers trapped in their cave—Jim stands to gain nothing from the lethal choice he is invited to make. Only the local natives—the hostages, their friends and families—stand to gain. Poor Jim is bound to lose, as will emerge in due course. In this respect, Jim is a bit like Sophie in William Styron's novel *Sophie's Choice*; whichever of her two children Sophie chooses to save from the Nazi gas chamber, she still stands to lose—the other one. (A crucial difference, of course, is that whereas Sophie is invited by the Nazi officer to choose to *save* one, the captain invites Jim to choose to *kill* one.)

II

We may as well begin by considering what advice the utilitarian would give Jim. Outcomes and their value alone matter for the utilitarian. So, in this case, we begin by concentrating on exactly two possible outcomes, those defined by the captain's offer. For the utilitarian, the preferred outcome is the one that involves as few dead as possible, discounted by the probability of that outcome. The fewest dead—an outcome with one dead hostage and 19 alive—is apparently the outcome only if Jim acts on the captain's offer. The other possible outcome begins with Jim's refusal to accept the captain's offer and ends with the firing squad killing all 20 hostages.

Bernard Williams comments that for the utilitarian, "obviously the right answer" is this: "Jim should kill the Indian." Why is this so "obviously" what a utilitarian would advise Jim to do? The answer must go like this: The utilitarian starts by defining right acts as whatever will yield the outcome with the greatest net balance of value over disvalue; utilitarians, in short, want us to act on the principle *Maximize Net Benefits*. Since human life is valued and is valuable, in this case the death of only one at Jim's hands is obviously a much better outcome than the death of all 20 at the hands of the firing squad. It is easy to see that a utilitarian might think in just this way and that, if he does, he will urge Jim to accept the captain's invitation to shoot one of the hostages. But I don't think the thoughtful utilitarian "obviously" gives this counsel, and it is useful to see why not.

If the probabilities of both outcomes are equal, then "obviously," as Williams says, the utilitarian prefers the first outcome to the second. Indeed, since the number of lives lost on the first outcome is so much smaller than on the second, the utilitarian would counsel Jim to shoot one hostage even if the probability of the preferred outcome is somewhat smaller than that of the alternative outcome.

But is this reasoning sound? I think not. First of all, there are many possible outcomes in this case—although each begins either with Jim's accepting the captain's offer or with Jim's refusing the offer. Whatever Jim's choice, neither outcome ends at that point. So how can the utilitarian insist on deciding what to do by reference to the consequences unless we carefully consider all the further consequences of the two alternatives open to Jim, whatever they are? As for which of the several possible outcome scenarios will turn out to be the actual outcome in this case, of course, we do not know, and neither does Jim. The utilitarian moral philosopher is equally ignorant. If, for the sake of argument, we decide temporarily to confine our thinking to the two outcomes so far identified, which of the two should we expect or predict? Which is the more likely, either on a priori or empirical grounds? We don't know this, either. It is all very well for the utilitarian to do his simple calculations in the manner I sketched a moment ago. But there is no guarantee that the other 19 go free if Jim kills one hostage. Likewise, there is no guarantee that nothing else of relevance will happen—but only if nothing else of relevance *does* happen is the apparently superior outcome as judged by the utilitarian principle "obviously" superior under that principle.

III

Let us look more closely at Jim's predicament in ways appropriate to trying to resolve it on utilitarian grounds. First of all, it does not lie in Jim's hands, much less in the act of his killing one hostage, for the desired result to come to pass. The most we can say is that Jim's killing some one hostage in the circumstances is a *necessary* condition of the apparently preferable outcome. But his killing that hostage certainly is not by itself *sufficient*; by itself, that killing cannot cause or bring about the desired outcome. Equally necessary to that outcome is the captain's keeping his promise to free the 19 after Jim kills the one. But ensuring that the captain keeps *his* promise is not within *Jim's* power. Nothing Jim can do could count as keeping the captain's promise. Worse than that, nothing Jim can do will ensure that the captain keeps his promise. (For instance, Jim cannot hold the captain to threat after shooting the one hostage, by saying to him, "If you don't keep your promise to let the 19 go free, I'll shoot you.") So between Jim's killing one hostage and the other 19 hostages going free there yawns a considerable gap.

Once the possibility that the captain is untrustworthy and might not keep his word occurs to the utilitarian, he must realize that he cannot "obviously" advise Jim to shoot one hostage. Instead, the utilitarian must consider giving Jim totally different advice, for instance, this: "Thank the captain politely for the invitation, but firmly decline it; then, having made some appropriate excuse, walk out of the clearing and back into the jungle whence you came." After all, it may be that the best interest of all concerned require the slaughter of these hostages; in no other way can the natives be galvanized into full-scale rebellion against an oppressive and tyrannical government, which if overthrown will be replaced by a better government. On the other hand, of course, if Jim rejects the captain's offer and tries to walk away, the natives gathered in the clearing, furious with his refusal to act as they want, may turn on him en masse and severely wound or even kill him—and, by enraging Pedro or the captain, bring on the slaughter of yet more of the natives. Jim has stumbled into a nightmarish dilemma, one in which his own life is suddenly at risk. Nothing in utilitarian moral thinking requires us to be blind to this fact; so, a utilitarian who, for whatever reason, fails to consider possible adverse consequences arising from Jim's pursuit of the apparently preferable alternative risks giving Jim very bad advice indeed.

IV

As this brief excursus shows, the utilitarian who would advise Jim cannot stop with identifying and comparing the merits of the two possible outcomes defined only in terms of accepting or declining the captain's offer, for either response to that offer has remoter consequences of varying likelihood and attractiveness. The utilitarian must consider all these further scenarios—among them those sketched above—however unpleasant they may be.

More than that, and as a second point, the utilitarian must

also consider the probability of each of the various branching possible outcomes in the circumstances. For example, what is the probability that, as soon as Jim shoots the hostage, this happens: The captain—instead of keeping his word—arrests Jim, accuses him of murder and Yankee arrogance to boot, and orders him summarily executed along with the rest of the hostages, lest he survive to tell tales that the capitain does not want made public. Or, to consider a different possibility, might it be that in reality the villagers are a tribe of thugs who for years have preyed on explorers, travellers, and government officials? Milder measures of remonstrance have been tried with them, but without success; now the tribe has fostered rebellion against the government in order to carry on its criminal activities, and the government's patience is understandably at an end. To teach the tribal thugs a lesson, the captain and his firing squad have been ordered to round up a random group and shoot them. If the firing squad does its duty, the rebellion and the thuggery in the district will substantially end, to the general benefit.

Why are these outcomes any less probable than the two main alternatives initially defined through the captain's offer? Jim cannot answer this question, and neither can the utilitarian who would advise him. Jim must act in virtually total ignorance of the relevant facts about the captain, the hostages, and the rest of the villagers—facts on which sound utilitarian advice depends. So the requisite calculations or estimates that would enable Jim to choose on empirical grounds among the various alternatives so far mentioned cannot be made, because there is no empirical information of the appropriate sort available. Does this mean that the utilitarian can give Jim no advice whatever? It certainly looks that way; advice from a utilitarian on how Jim ought to act is completely dependent on empirical information, in this case as in every other.

Some might be tempted to help the utilitarian aiming to advise Jim along lines suggested by remarks of John Stuart Mill's that gave rise forty years ago to so-called *rule utilitarianism*. Instead of trying to calculate the probabilities of the consequences of the two alternative *acts* open to Jim, the rule utilitarian advises Jim to act according to whatever *rule* would maximize net benefits if people in similar situations were generally to act on that rule. For simplicity, let's confine our attention to two rules, each based on generalizations about human conduct in situations like Jim's, as follows:

1. The captain is a man of his word, as befits his status as an army officer, so Jim need not worry overmuch either about adverse consequences for him from acting on the captain's offer or about the captain reneging on the offer after Jim has killed the one hostage. As a rule, army captains can be taken at their word.

2. The captain is an utterly untrustworthy scoundrel, indeed unstable, as is shown by his willingness to kill hostages at random *pour encourager les autres*, by his groundless decision to treat Jim as an honored guest, by his frivolous invitation to Jim to kill any one hostage of his choosing, and by his (apparent) promise not to kill any more hostages despite his duty to repress rebellion in the jungle. As a rule, scoundrels are not to be trusted, and one deals with them at one's peril.

Any utilitarian who thinks that Jim "obviously" ought to take the captain's offer must believe that the value of the consequences discounted by their probability stemming from acting on the first generalization is at least somewhat greater than those stemming from acting on the second generalization. But why does the utilitarian think this? Why should we think *either* of these generalizations is more likely than the other? No doubt the world would be a better place if we could take army officers at their word. But can Jim trust *this* army captain to the requisite degree? In the circumstances, for which Jim has no precedent in any of his experience, he has no empirical basis on which to reason by reference to the first generalization any more than he does to reason by reference to the second generalization.

I conclude from this discussion that Bernard Williams was wrong in thinking that the utilitarian advising Jim would "obviously" advise him to shoot the one hostage in order to save the 19 others. All that is obvious, if anything is, is that the utilitarian cannot easily give any useful counsel to Jim. With that, I leave the utilitarian behind us—except to add, by way of anticipation, that the outcome Williams thought was "obviously" favored by the utilitarian may in fact be the best outcome after all, although for entirely nonutilitarian reasons.

V

Let us begin afresh by confronting the fact—and it does seem to be a fact—that Jim, if he shoots one of the hostages, is not merely killing that hostage: He is murdering him. However you wish to define "murder," any plausible definition will apply to what Jim does if he shoots one of the hostages in order to kill him. The fact that he acts with the permission of the captain (and, to that extent, with the captain's authority); that he kills in order to save many innocent lives; that he personally gains nothing from the killing; that he does not kill as an act of revenge or out of any other discreditable motive; that he kills with deep regrets (perhaps even with revulsion at what he does)—none of these facts alters the primary fact: If and when he kills a hostage, he commits murder.

In this respect, the death Jim causes, if he chooses to cause any, is not the same as the killings discussed in the first chapter, the drownings at sea that Holmes caused. At worst, those killings were manslaughter; at best they were homicides justifiable on grounds of necessity. But no necessity can be invoked to justify the killing Jim causes, if he chooses to cause any. Nor is the killing Jim causes, if he chooses to cause any, quite the same as the killing discussed in the second chapter, the murder of Whetmore by his fellow spelunkers trapped in the cave. For the natural necessity that is such a conspicuous part of the circumstances in which the drownings at sea and the killing and cannibalism in the cave occur is completely missing in this case. Here in the jungle clearing, it is not necessary for anyone to die. All can survive, if only the right people decide to act in the right way.

Murder—even of a stranger, even at the invitation of one in authority, even in an effort to save lives of the innocent—is not an act to be undertaken lightly. Mindful of the distinction between justifying and excusing the one who causes another harm, do those who want Jim to shoot the hostage do better if they try to understand Jim's killing as an excusable homicide, rather than as a justified one? It will be recalled that in the Holmes case I argued that it is implausible to try to excuse Holmes's throwing men overboard in order to increase the likelihood that the others in the boat would survive; rather, Holmes's only defense is that the killings he caused were justified. In the case of the speluncean explorers, I argued that it is not only impossible to excuse the killing of Whetmore; it is also impossible to justify it.

What should we say in this case? Surely, the kinds of circumstances and intentions in and out of which Jim would act were he to shoot a hostage are not any of those that would *excuse* him for what he was doing. He does not, for example, shoot to hit a nearby target only to kill an innocent hostage instead. He does not shoot a hostage after taking careful aim, thinking all the while he's shooting at only a picture of a hostage. And so on we go down the list of accident, mistake, ignorance, loss of self-control, incapacity, and the rest of the excusing conditions. Nor does he act under duress. No one holds him to threat as he decides whether to shoot a hostage.

VI

In this connection, consider just how different the situation would be if instead of offering Jim the chance to shoot one hostage in order to save the other 19, the captain had threatened Jim by saying, "Either you shoot one of the hostages, or we'll shoot you." In this case, Jim might well shoot the hostage and plead life-threatening duress, an excuse if anything is an excuse, some would say. Is that what we should say in such a case? Or—to pile on the agony—suppose that Jim had arrived in the jungle clearing with his two small children, and the captain, after making his offer to Jim, says threateningly: "Either you kill a hostage, or we'll kill your two young children." If Jim killed a hostage under duress, as in either of these two hypothetical situations, he would be no less a murderer than in the initial case. For (unlike the fictional James Bond) Jim has no "license to kill" others—not even a perfect stranger to save other innocent third parties, such as his own children.

If kill he must to save innocent lives, then let him try to kill the unjust aggressor (or let him offer himself as a sacrifice). But if no such preventive killing is possible (and if his sacrificial offer is rejected), then Jim must take the awful consequences of his plight. He simply has no right to murder one innocent person in the hope that thereby he will persuade another not to murder other innocent persons; he has no right to try to preserve himself or those dear to him by violating the right to life of another. We must not cave in under such threats.

Of course, some will say that in the two variant scenarios sketched above, in which if Jim kills, he does so under duress, the life-threatening circumstances in which he acts at least mitigate his culpability and downgrade the criminal homicide he causes from murder to manslaughter. For in these cases as hypothesized, the threat he faces is "of present, imminent and impending death or serious bodily harm"—although not harm to him, and the law if not morality recognizes that such threats provide an *excuse* for committing what would otherwise be a crime. Legal authorities agree on this much, but they are divided over whether duress can serve to excuse a crime as serious as homicide; some argue that if some degree of duress can excuse a crime, then greater duress can excuse even murder, whereas others say if the crime is murder, then duress, no matter how extreme, can only mitigate the severity of the deserved punishment. Moral reflection, I suspect, will leave us equally divided over this point. But that need not trouble us in the present context, since if Jim kills a hostage he does so at another's invitation, not under duress. Debating how Jim should act if under a threat radically changes the scenario with which we began, so much so that we need pay no further attention to the idea.

Can Jim take refuge in the principle that he kills to achieve a good end? That in choosing the lesser evil he does evil in order to achieve a greater good? Perhaps he can, but the point is not a new one. This principle seems to be merely another version of the consequentialist principle relied on by the utilitarian I discussed earlier. The only obvious difference is that this principle admits without disguise that the act to be justified is itself an evil act—it is, as I have been insisting, an act of murder, and murder is surely wrong—whereas the utilitarian principle either conceals or ignores this fact by focusing not on what Jim does but on all and only the probable and foreseeable consequences of the options open to him.

VII

How does Jim fare if he decides to accept the captain's offer and seeks vindication under the *Doctrine of Double Effect?* This principle is best known for the way it permits a doctor to end a pregnancy in certain special cases without opening the door generally to abortion in other cases. The surgeon, seeking to save the life of the pregnant woman, knows that by excising the fetus (as in an ectopic pregnancy) or the uterus (as when it is cancerous), which is necessary to save maternal life, ends the life of the unborn. But the intended effect of what the surgeon does is life-saving (for the mother), not death-dealing (for the unborn), even though death of the fetus is one of the foreseeable and foreseen consequences of the surgery.

Thus, the principle (in one of its many formulations) says

this: Whenever a given action has two effects, one good and the other evil, it is morally permissible to perform the action and to let the evil occur if and only if, first, one acts with the intention to bring about the good, not the evil, although the evil is foreseen; second, the action itself must be good or at least not evil; and third, the good effect of the action must bring about at least as much good as the evil effect brings about evil.

What does this principle tell us about Jim's killing a hostage? The first condition is satisfied, since in accepting and carrying out the captain's offer Jim acts only with the intention to bring about good—sparing the lives of 19 hostages. As for the third condition, it too is probably satisfied, at least on a charitable reading, since the foreseen evil incurred—one definite death—is outweighed by the greater evil averted—19 deaths (provided, of course, this evil really is averted). But we must not make too much of any uncertainty on this point; in the abortion case, the surgeon may very well operate on the mother to save her life, killing the unborn (or letting it die) in the process, and yet fail to save the mother's life. Even so, no one would argue from that regrettable outcome in conjunction with accepting the Doctrine of Double Effect to the conclusion that the surgeon ought not to have tried to do what he did.

The second of the three defining conditions under this principle, however, must give Jim pause. The action he is required to take in order to carry out the captain's offer is, as we have said before, murder. And surely murdering the innocent is as evil an action as one can perform. The death by murder at Jim's hands of the one hostage is not an unintended consequence of Jim's actions. Jim may not *like* that consequence, but unless he intends to shoot to kill he cannot seriously be said to be intending the primary effect, either, namely bringing about the good end.

So the verdict of this inquiry has to be that Jim cannot turn the murder he would commit into a morally permissible killing by appeal to the Doctrine of Double Effect.

VIII

Let us suppose that, influenced by the failure of utilitarian counsels to direct him and by the counsel against accepting the captain's offer that arises from considering Double Effect, Jim refuses the captain's offer, and the captain proceeds as he said he would and has the firing squad kill all 20 hostages. Should Jim now judge himself to be at least partially responsible for these 20 deaths? Does the captain's invitation and Jim's refusal to accept it *make* him in any way at fault for the 20 deaths? When the hostages are shot, if they are, should he feel guilty, because he *is* guilty of these deaths, at least to the extent that his failure to do what he could have tried to do makes him guilty? After all, he could have murdered one hostage in the hope that the captain would keep his promise. He could have tried, we might say. Instead, for whatever reason—most likely, his scruples against killing another human being—he chooses not to shoot.

Some will now argue that, far from Jim's refusal to commit murder adding to his moral bank account, his refusal shows he is under a self-deceiving illusion of innocence. He is to be severely faulted for his scruples, since his refusal to soil his hands is nothing but a misguided effort to preserve his own high principles, quite out of place in the circumstances. This objection emerges with greater clarity if we think how those who want Jim to shoot the hostage might react if he did shoot—only to have the captain break his promise and have the other 19 shot as well. "After all," these sympathetic critics would say, "Jim may not have done everything imaginable to save the other 19. But he did all that he could reasonably do in the circumstances. He did try, and that's all we have a right to expect of him or anyone in such circumstances. So he bears no responsibility for their deaths. True, Jim is responsible for the death of the hostage he intentionally killed, but in any case that death is justified. It's not his fault that the captain failed to keep his word. He's certainly not responsible, and a fortiori not to be blamed, for the additional 19 deaths the captain ordered."

But is this right? Jim might try to reinforce the conclusion by arguing as follows:

> Look, there is a profound difference between my responsibility for murdering a hostage if I take up the captain's offer, and my alleged responsibility for the captain's decision to order the killing of all the hostages. There is a direct and unmistakable *causal* relationship between my shooting a hostage and the death of that hostage; but there is no such causal relationship—not even an indirect or hidden one—between my refusing to shoot a hostage and the captain's having all 20 shot and killed. It is the firing squad, carrying out the captain's order, that causes those twenty deaths, not I. So how can I be held even partially responsible for what the captain and the firing squad do? Like me, they can choose and decide what to do and what not to do, and for such choices they are to be held responsible, morally and legally. If all 20 hostages are killed, then it is the firing squad that causes those deaths, not I. If it were up to me, none of the hostages would die; but all that is

up to me is whether I will kill one. Were I to kill one I would be fully responsible for his death. But I will not murder him on the strength of the captain's bizarre offer, and I cannot be held responsible for any murders that others cause because I refuse to commit murder.

If Jim had been so fortunate as to have studied philosophy in the 1950s at Oxford, he might have put the gist of his reply to his critics as follows:

> Look, if you think I share responsibility for the deaths of the 20 hostages when I refuse to take up the captain's offer, you're just being misled by the superficial similarity between two conditional propositions. The first of these conditionals says:
>
> 1. If I pull the trigger, then the gun fires.
>
> The second says:
>
> 2. If I refuse the captain's offer, then 20 hostages die.
>
> Now [Jim continues], as the philosopher J. L. Austin might have put it, the "if" in these two conditionals is not the same sort of "if." The first proposition states a true causal conditional; by my pulling the trigger, I cause the gun to fire. But the second proposition is not a causal conditional at all. By my refusing the offer I do not *cause* anyone to die—I don't *cause* anything at all. Instead, the captain uses my refusal as *his* reason for carrying out *his* threat. To think that my refusal causes any deaths is just absurd, just as it would be preposterous for the captain, upon hearing my refusal, to say, "Well, that leaves me with no choice. It's entirely out of my hands. All the hostages must now die, and it's your refusal that causes them to be shot by my firing squad."
>
> The same point [Jim goes on] can be made if we shift from thinking about "cause" to thinking about "*be*cause." Upon hearing my refusal, it would be utterly preposterous for the captain to say, "Well, all the hostages must now die because

> you refused my offer." Nonsense. If the hostages *must* now be killed, it is *because* the captain and the firing squad under his orders have decided to kill them.
>
> If [Jim concludes] you grant—as you must—that neither "cause" nor "because" connects my refusal of the captain's offer to the deaths of the 20 hostages, then I cannot be responsible for their deaths. My actions no more make me responsible for their deaths than do the actions of the hostages' families and friends. Responsibility for dead hostages rests entirely with those who gave the orders to kill them and with those who carried out such orders. I did neither.

At this point, those who think it best for Jim to shoot the hostage might reply in a vein popularized in recent years by many philosophers, saying:

> Jim, you are attaching unreasonable weight to the distinction between killing and letting die, and quite forgetting that if you refuse to kill one you are letting 20 die. That is, you are letting the captain and his firing squad go ahead and kill all twenty. But there is no morally significant difference between acts through which one kills and acts through which one lets others die.

I would hope Jim would not be persuaded by this argument, even if its major premise is true.

Even if, that is, it is true that there is no morally significant difference between killing and letting die, it ought to be clear that in Jim's situation this point has no relevance. The reason it has no relevance is that the point of denying any moral significance to the distinction presupposes that it is within one's power to prevent a death that one nevertheless refuses to prevent, just as it is within one's power not to cause a death which one nevertheless causes—and it is precisely this power that Jim lacks.

Consider in this light the case of 20 natives struggling in a deep and swift-flowing river. Jim has at hand just one life preserver; if he throws it into the midst of the natives, it could save one. But he refuses to throw the life preserver, and all 20 drown. Jim, we might well say in this case, let at least one of the 20 die without trying to save that one.

But is that what he does in the jungle clearing when he refuses to murder a hostage? I think not. When Jim is on the riverbank holding the life preserver, it is within his power to keep—or at least to try to keep—one native from drowning. But as we have already seen, it is not within Jim's power to keep the firing squad from killing all or even any of the hostages. So his refusal to murder one in the hope of saving 19 cannot be construed as Jim's letting all 20 die; Jim no more lets hostages die by refusing to kill one than Sophie in Styron's novel *Sophie's Choice* lets one of her children die by choosing to protect the other. It is not within her power to protect both.

IX

Perhaps at this point someone will want to ask what role the numbers ought to play in resolving Jim's dilemma. Consider two variations on the original story. In the first, there are only two hostages before the firing squad, and the captain says to Jim: "If you shoot one, I'll let the other go; but if you don't, then I'll order the firing squad to shoot both as originally planned." In the second version, there are 200 hostages, and the captain says to Jim: "If you shoot one, I'll let the other 199 go; but if you don't, then all 200 will be shot as originally planned." Is there any reason, more or less, for Jim to shoot in one of these cases than there is for him to shoot in the original scenario, in which if he shoots one he does so in order to spare the lives of 19?

One must admit that the more the numbers go up, the more one is tempted to encourage Jim to accept the captain's offer and all the risks it entails. Wouldn't *you* commit one murder if by doing so you could save the whole human race from extermination? Or, to make the example more precisely parallel to Jim's situation, wouldn't you be willing to murder an innocent stranger, chosen essentially at random, in the hope that by doing so you increased the likelihood that the whole human race (yourself included) and all living things would be released from bondage to a madman who threatened—and had the power to carry out the threat—to kill everyone unless . . . ? Surely I am not alone in being tempted to say, "I would be willing to murder in such a case."

The issue here can be formulated more abstractly: Is our rejection of certain principles, such as the principle that it is wrong to do evil in a good cause, so firm and absolute that even in this extreme case we would be unwilling to murder? In cases such as this, in which we face a choice between grave evils, is it not the counsel of wisdom to choose the lesser evil—at least, when the greater evil is *so* much greater?

If we think like this, we in effect accept the prevailing answer to what is known in the recent philosophical literature as the Trolley Problem. Imagine that you stand at a switching lever on the trolley line. Coming down the track is a runaway trolley, headed for a group of 20 people trapped in a culvert. If the trolley continues, it will hit and kill all the people in the culvert. But there is a side track, on which a car is stalled with the driver trapped inside. You see the two possible outcomes. All you can do is leave the switch alone or throw it; if you throw the switch you send the trolley down the side track, where it will kill the one person trapped in the car. What should you do? The cautious will say that, knowing no more about the situation and the trapped persons than has been given so far, you are permitted to throw the switch, and so you may throw it if you want to. A few will argue that you ought to flip a coin to decide, since the losses are equal in both cases, because there's no significance to aggregating lives lost in such cases—all that is lost by each person is one life, and the losses do not add to more just because more lives are lost. But most of us would still say that in these circumstances, one ought to act to save the most possible. And that involves choosing to cause one to be killed rather than choosing to let 20 be killed. We have here as close to a paradigm case as we can get for when the numbers count.

But, of course, this case sheds very little light on Jim's plight in the jungle. For in the Trolley Problem natural necessity guarantees that some will die no matter what you do; your role is either to let nature take its course—in which case 20 die—or to intervene and reduce the number who die to the minimum: one. And if you do intervene, so that one is killed, it is guaranteed that the 20 in the culvert are spared. In Jim's situation, however, since the captain and the firing squad are not mindless mechanisms rolling out of control down the tracks that lead inevitably to killing one or killing 20, there is no guarantee that Jim's killing one will spare 19: Natural necessity does not rule.

The sharp difference between the Trolley Problem and

Jim's plight underscores the difference between cases in which, we might say, nothing but the numbers matter, and other cases—such as Jim's—in which this is only one consideration among several.

X

So far, we have looked at what Jim ought to do mainly from his point of view, as it were. We have tried to think through how Jim might view the decision-making challenge he faces. But we must also look at how Jim's possible courses of action strike the 20 hostages who are at risk, and their families and friends. As they see it, there are four possible outcomes, because Jim's decision to accept or reject the captain's offer is independent of the captain's decision to keep or break his word. Suppose Jim rejects the offer and the captain's promise is moot; anything might happen, including killing some of the hostages. Suppose instead Jim rejects and the captain keeps his word; then all 20 hostages die. As a third alternative, suppose Jim accepts and the captain keeps his word; then only one dies. Finally, suppose Jim accepts but the captain breaks his word; then, again, anything might happen.

Suppose you were one of the hostages. Which alternative would you prefer? What would you tell Jim he ought to do, were you to choose behind a veil of ignorance the principle on which he should act? (A veil of ignorance, if there were such a thing, would guarantee that one does not know how a principle affects any given person, including oneself, and therefore one cannot choose among alternative principles behind a veil of ignorance by reference to which alternative promotes selfish advantage.) Surely, you would want Jim to act so as to leave as few as possible of your group dead, and to respect each life equally—and thus to act so that whoever is killed is at least chosen randomly. Given that, you would prefer the third alternative to the others (if Jim shoots one hostage and the captain lets the others go free, each hostage has 19 chances out of 20 of not being the one chosen at random to be killed—the best you can hope for). So, you want Jim to accept the offer and kill one hostage, even though you cannot know whether the captain will keep his word.

Thus, you have two reasons for choosing the third alternative. First, you would hope that someone else would be the unlucky one shot by Jim—after all, it probably won't be you, since the probability you will be chosen is only 0.05; second, you would hope that the captain will keep his word, so that—if your luck holds again—you're set free. Now, each of the 20 hostages in principle ought to accept this reasoning; it is reasoning they could in theory unanimously endorse, because it favors none of the hostages over the others. On such reasoning, ignoring all other considerations, the hostages and their families and friends ought to tell Jim to go ahead and shoot one of the hostages—which is exactly what we were told in the original scenario they were "obviously begging" Jim to do.

Encouraged by this, some will argue that since it is the hostages whose lives are at stake, Jim ought to do what these potential victims want him to do. Since Jim is no fool, he can see exactly how the natives would reason in the manner sketched above. So, it is mere squeamishness on his part—these critics will say—if he refuses to shoot one hostage at random, knowing that this is what all the hostages want, and that it is perfectly reasonable in the circumstances for them to want this. Although none of the hostages, evidently, is willing to offer himself to Jim as a sacrificial victim for the sake of the rest, all are willing to let Jim choose one of their number for this role. What they want him to do ought to prevail over any other reasoning or preference, because—it will be argued—it is the hostages whose lives are at stake, and they therefore have the right to decide what risks they ought to run in the circumstances.

The unanimous desire of the hostages that Jim accept the captain's offer also has a significant effect on what has been one of the fixed points of the discussion so far. I have said more than once that if Jim acts on the captain's offer, what he does is *murder* one of the hostages. But is that really so? After all, whichever hostage Jim decides to kill—if he decides to kill any—will be someone who has in effect already given Jim his consent to being killed. If that is so, then how can it still be murder if Jim shoots that hostage?

Well, it *is* still murder, if you define "murder" as willful, deliberate killing of another. Under this definition, euthanasia and physician-assisted suicide are murder, too. Even when consent is fully voluntary and rational, consent to die at the hands of another has until recently rarely been accepted by courts of law as a defense to the charge of murder; the possibility of abuse of such a defense is too obvious to need discussion. However, just as many of us today (including me) are prepared to reconceptualize murder—and change the law accordingly—so that rational and voluntary consent to another's help in dying justifies, say, a doctor in rendering such help, so some will want to insist that Jim, too, has been authorized by his victim to be killed so that the rest can go free. On this view of the matter, Jim's killing a hostage seems no longer to be murder, because it is justifiable homicide.

Suppose we grant this much. If we do, some will insist that the manifest prior consent of the hostages provides only *permission* to Jim to kill a hostage; it does not yet show that Jim *ought* to kill a hostage. (And it certainly does not impose any duty or obligation on him to shoot one of the hostages.) Hence, the hostage's consent by itself does not suffice to show that Jim is fully *justified* if he decides to kill a hostage. (In general, one is not justified in doing something merely because one is morally permitted to do it; it is often quite undesirable to do what neither law nor morality forbids, for instance, overeating or excessive consumption of alcohol.) What, then, is required in this context to bridge the gap between permission and justification? To this question, alas, there is no precise answer. We do not have an algorithm that yields a definite answer when all and only the relevant reasons are specified, or a morality machine into which we can type in the information about a given problem case, such as Jim's, then press a sequence of keys, and get a printout with the morally correct verdict.

XI

Here, at last, we confront the most difficult aspect of Jim's predicament from the moral point of view. If Jim really does not want to accept the captain's offer, believing that it is an invitation to commit murder—never mind the untold risks for him and the others in the bargain—then yielding to the natives's preference that he nevertheless shoot one hostage amounts to becoming their tool, an instrument of their will.

The idea is not unfamiliar to us, nor perhaps wholly repellent. In the Bible we read, "Let not my will but thine be done." This declaration, however, is addressed by Jesus to his Father; the 20 hostages and the throng of their friends and families hardly speak to Jim with parental, much less divine, authority. Indeed, their will has no authority over him, except as he chooses to allow it.

Well, why should Jim *not* let himself be an instrument of their will? Why should he set his absolute scruples against murder in a very good cause at higher value than he sets their collective rational preference? Is he not vulnerable to criticism on grounds of self-indulgence if he ranks his integrity, such as it is, higher in the scale of moral values than their desire to live—a desire not marred by any lack of innocence on their part? I am not sure that there is any decisive answer to be given to these questions.

At the end of the day, some will think it best for Jim to refuse the captain's offer, secure in the knowledge that he causes no deaths even if he is necessarily troubled by the knowledge that he has not done everything reasonably within his power to prevent all the 20 deaths. Others will think it best if Jim accepts the captain's offer, discounting his own integrity as hyperscrupulosity, secure in the knowledge that he did everything within reason to prevent all 20 deaths from occurring (even if his effort fails) and that he did what the hostages themselves wanted him to do.

For my part, I cannot carry the analysis of this case any further; unlike the killings Holmes caused, which I argued were justified, and unlike the killing of Whetmore, which I argued was not justified, the right solution to Jim's dilemma eludes me. With that confession, I leave it for you to decide: What, if you were Jim, would you think you ought to do?

PRINCIPLES AND GOALS

The Utilitarian Principle: Among alternative acts open to the agent, the right act is the act with the maximum net benefit suitably discounted by its probability.

Maximize Net Benefits: The principle of utility in brief form.

Rule Utilitarianism: Act on the rule that among the alternative rules relevant in a given situation is the one most likely to result in the greatest net benefit if it were generally adopted.

Choose the Lesser Evil: Another corollary of the principle of utility.

The Doctrine of Double Effect: Whenever a given action has two effects, one good and the other evil, it is morally permissible to perform the action and to let the evil occur if and only if, first, one acts with the intention to bring about the good, not the evil; second, the action itself is good or at least not evil; and third, the good effect of the action brings about at least as much good as the evil effect brings about evil.

Veil of Ignorance: Act on whatever principle you would choose behind a veil of ignorance, assuming that you would choose to maximize your self-interest.

Subordination of Self: Make yourself the willing instrument of the will of others insofar as it is their interests that are primarily affected by your action.

APPENDIX

The Historical Background of Casuistry

The term "casuistry" is derived from *casus,* Latin for "case," and refers to the study of individual "cases of conscience" in which more than one settled moral principle (or perhaps none) applies. More broadly, casuistry is the use of the "method of cases" in the attempt to bring ethical reflections to bear on problems requiring the decision and action of some moral agent. A casuist is thus one who is trained to provide such counsel. Accordingly, casuistry is a branch of applied ethics. Since the seventeenth century, however, the term has often been used in a derogatory sense, as though casuistry were a species of sophistical reasoning by means of which almost any conduct could apparently be deemed permissible, provided only that one is ingenious enough in exploiting exceptions and special circumstances.

For the casuist, the solution to a morally problematic case is obtained by comparing and contrasting its features with various paradigm cases whose moral status is settled. Solutions to the problem cases rely both on moral principles or maxims that express the received wisdom concerning such paradigms and on analogies to them. The plurality of principles is a source of their actual or potential conflict, but their general reliability otherwise is taken for granted. Hence, casuistry as a method of practical reasoning tends to rely on some form of intuitionism as well as on some set of moral norms more or less beyond dispute.

The governing idea of casuistry is expressed in the second-order maxim that "circumstances alter cases." As Thomas Aquinas wrote (1275): "The human act ought to vary according to diverse conditions of persons, time and other circumstances: this is the entire matter of morality."[1] The method of cases is designed to take these "diverse conditions" into account. This is to be contrasted both with mechanical application of rigid rules of conduct and with the attempt to ground moral decision making in some grand theory of the good or the right.

Casuistry is a natural outgrowth of three features of Aristotle's *Nichomachean Ethics* (ca. 330 B.C.E.). First, Aristotle took it for granted that persons have a grasp of the principles of right conduct, based on their socialization as members of a human community. He also argued that it is impossible to secure theoretical precision in practical matters, and so ethical reasoning should not aspire to the rigor appropriate to a true science. Finally, practical wisdom (Aristotelian *phronesis*) is essential to right conduct; it can be obtained only by critical reflection on actual experience in confronting the diverse problems that human life presents.

1. Quoted in Albert R. Johnson and Stephen Toulmin, *The Abuse of Casuistry: A History of Moral Reasoning,* Berkeley, University of California Press, 1988, p. 135. My remarks in this essay are much indebted to this volume.

Casuistry (although not under that name) was taught for centuries as part of Greco-Roman rhetoric. A standard exercise required the student to propose and defend a solution to a practical problem by means of arguments and counterarguments in which various moral principles and solutions to analogous cases would be integrated for maximum persuasive effect. Cicero's *De Officiis* (ca. 44 B.C.E.) provided later generations with a partial catalogue of famous cases in which either a conflict of duties or a conflict between duty and expediency needed to be resolved. Thus, later casuistry can be seen as a systematic approach to ethical problems derived from Ciceronian rhetoric.

Rabbinic *pilpul* and Roman common law also influenced moral casuistry independently of classical rhetoric. Weighing relevant principles, arguing from paradigm cases, distinguishing apparently contrary conclusions in prior cases—all are familiar methods both in the resolution of disputes through the common law and in Talmudic commentary and interpretation. Among Christians, the need to reconcile the Mosaic law with the examples and counsels in the Gospels in order to provide guidance for daily life made the development of casuistical reasoning by the clergy all but inevitable. These legal and pastoral elements were combined in the development of canon law and penitential discipline during the Middle Ages.

From 1200 through 1650, the teaching and practice of casuistry flourished in Europe. The *Summa de sacramentis et animae conciliis* (ca. 1191) by Peter Cantor of Paris was perhaps the first true casuistic treatise. With the founding of the Society of Jesus in 1534, casuistry dominated pastoral (moral) theology. Treatises in which hundreds, even thousands, of cases were presented and discussed became commonplace. One of the most influential was the *Enchiridion* (1556) of Martin Navarrus. In 1600, the Jesuit Juan Azor published his *Institutionum Moralium,* nearly four thousand pages long, in which he declared "all questions of conscience are briefly treated." The monumental *Resolutiones morales* (1629–59) by Antonius Diana, "the Prince of Casuists," discussed some 20 thousand cases in 10 volumes.

A principal factor in the decline of casuistry, leading to its worst abuses, was the doctrine that if a practical opinion or counsel is probably true, it is permitted to follow it, even though it is more probable that the opposite opinion is true. This thesis, known subsequently as "probabilism," was first enunciated by Bartolome Medina in 1577. Hitherto, the predominant view had been the obvious one that where there were divergent opinions on how to act, differing in their likelihood of being correct, the path of *prudentia* (practical reason) was to follow the more probable opinion. This was the *via tutior,* the "safer way."

In practice, probabilism often meant that if persons wanted to act in a manner contrary to the best counsels, they were free to do so (that is, if they did not violate any moral duty), provided there was some plausible ground for doubting that one really was forbidden to act in the desired manner. Such a ground could be either "extrinsic," based on the opinion of some authoritative moral thinker, or "intrinsic," based on a good reason or argument, whatever its source.

The underlying purpose of probabilism has been said to be "to lighten the burden of conscience on the unscrupulous and troubled."[2] But the less scrupulous could use probabilism to serve selfish interests, thus deservedly incurring the charge of

2. Johnson and Toulmin, *The Abuse of Casuistry,* p. 168.

"laxism" and thereby bringing the very practice of casuistry into disrepute.

The disappearance of penitential discipline under Protestantism, combined with the criticism of laxism from within the Roman church itself, weakened the practice and authority of casuistry.[3] But the truly fatal blow was delivered by Blaise Pascal in his *Lettres Provinciales* (1656–57). As a Jansenist, convinced that the path of Christian rectitude involves strict compliance with the pure spirit of the Gospels, Pascal was hostile to the probabilist casuistry taught by the more worldly Jesuits. Writing anonymously, he mocked it unmercifully and exposed to ridicule the moral laxity of its diverse counsels.

However unfair a caricature of the actual methods and principles of casuistry Pascal's attack may have been, it succeeded in discrediting the entire practice. Henceforth, little more than faint echoes of casuistry would be found in the ethical writings of the leading philosophers outside the clerical tradition, such as Kant and J. S. Mill. By the end of the nineteenth century, with ethical pluralism and intuitionism on the defensive generally, Henry Sidgwick could write five hundred pages on *The Methods of Ethics* (1874) and dismiss casuistry in a sentence.

Thanks to the growing importance in the 1970s of applied ethics and of professional ethics in particular, a "new casuistry" has appeared in which the old "method of cases" has been revived and modified.[4]

3. For further discussion of casuistry during this period, see Edmund Leites, ed., *Conscience and Casuistry in Early Modern Europe,* Cambridge, Cambridge University Press, 1988.

4. See, for example, Christopher W. Gowans, ed., *Moral Dilemmas,* New York, Oxford University Press, 1987.

Notes

CHAPTER ONE

Page 7: *United States v. Holmes.* This case was tried in Philadelphia in 1842 before the federal Circuit Court for the Eastern District of Pennsylvania. The text of the reported case on which my discussion is based will be found in volume 26 of *Federal Cases,* starting at p. 360; the reporter was John William Wallace. The case has frequently been reprinted, in whole or in part, e.g., in Philip E. Davis, ed., *Moral Duty and Legal Responsibility,* New York, Appleton-Century-Crofts, 1966, pp. 102–18, where I first read it. It has been much discussed in the philosophical and legal literature, e.g., by Edmund Cahn, *The Moral Decision: Right and Wrong in the Light of American Law,* Bloomington, Indiana University Press, 1956, pp. 61–71. The details of the case, along with other similar cases, have been examined in A. W. B. Simpson, *Cannibalism and the Common Law: The Story of the Tragic Last Voyage of the Mignonette and the Strange Legal Proceedings to*

Which It Gave Rise, Chicago, University of Chicago Press, 1984; chapter 9, "The *William Brown* and the *Euxine,*" is largely devoted to the *Holmes* case. I have relied on Simpson's account for some of the details in my version of the facts. A fuller but less accessible account of the case will be found in "The Trial of Alexander W. Holmes," in John D. Lawson, ed., *American State Trials,* 17 vols., St. Louis, Mo., Thomas, 1914–36, vol. 1, pp. 368–439. In the 1970s, a movie of the case was made for television, starring Martin Sheen as Seaman Holmes.

Page 9: goal versus principle. Following Ronald Dworkin, one can contrast a goal as the end or outcome one aims at, with a principle as a constraint on how that goal may be pursued. See Dworkin's "Model of Rules" (1967) in his *Taking Rights Seriously,* Cambridge, Harvard University Press, 1977, pp. 22–23. However, not all the principles I cite function in this manner.

Page 10: Streicher, Calley, and the defense of superior orders. The defense of superior orders has been much discussed in two contexts: the Nuremberg trials of the major Nazi war criminals, including Julius Streicher, in 1946, and the court martial in 1971 of two U.S. Army officers, Lieutenant William Calley and Captain Ernest Medina, for the massacre of civilians in South Vietnam. See, respectively, Robert E. Conot, *Justice at Nuremberg,* New York, Harper & Row, 1983, and Seymour Hersh, *My Lai Four—A Report on the Massacre and Its Aftermath,* New York, Random House, 1970. Although Holmes hardly engaged in a massacre, his situation is akin to that of the enlisted men at My Lai in Calley's platoon, none of whom was court martialed, presumably because all had a defense of superior orders. Note also the South

African case from the Boer War, in which Judge Sir Richard Solomon said: "[I]f a soldier honestly believes he is doing his duty in obeying the commands of his superior, and if the orders are not so manifestly illegal that he must or ought to have known they are unlawful, the private soldier would be protected by the orders of his superior officer." Quoted in J. C. Smith and Brian Hogan, *Criminal Law,* 4th ed., London, Butterworth, 1978, p. 210. The topic is briefly discussed by Michael Walzer, *Just and Unjust Wars,* New York, Basic Books, 1977, pp. 309–16; see also the sources he cites.

Page 12: Sole Means Necessary to the End. This consideration is not to be confused with the more sophisticated Sole-Means Principle for Permissibility, formulated and discussed by Judith Thomson in her excellent book, *The Realm of Rights,* Cambridge, Harvard University Press, 1990, p. 108. Her principle reads: "If the only means X has of doing beta is doing alpha, then it would be permissible for X to do beta if and only if it would be permissible for X to do alpha."

Page 14: justification versus excuse. I have relied on the account of this distinction made familiar to philosophers by J. L. Austin in his "A Plea for Excuses" (1956), in his *Philosophical Papers,* Oxford, Clarendon Press, 1961, pp. 175–77.

Page 18: Kantian Condition. What in the text I call the Kantian Condition Kant called "the practical imperative," the second version of his categorical imperative: "Act in such a way that you treat humanity, whether in your own person or in the person of another, always at the same time as an end and never simply as a means." Immanuel Kant, *Grounding for the Metaphysics of Morals* (1785) tr. James Ellington, Indianapolis, Hackett, 1981, p. 36.

Page 20: veil of ignorance. Popularized by John Rawls, *A*

Theory of Justice, Cambridge, Harvard University Press, 1971, pp. 136–41. As he points out, the idea "is so natural a condition [on fairly adopting fair principles] that something like it must have occurred to many." However, the only prior use of the idea he cites is by John C. Harsanyi, "Cardinal Utility in Welfare Economics and in the Theory of Risk-Taking," *Journal of Political Economy*, 61 (1953), 434–35.

Page 21: Captain Oates. His story is told in Robert F. Scott, *Scott's Last Expedition*, vol. 1, London, J. Murray, 1935, p. 462.

Page 23: fair lotteries. The role of lotteries in deciding fair distribution of risks, benefits, and burdens, is discussed in Barbara Goodwin, *Justice by Lottery*, Chicago: University of Chicago Press, 1992; see especially pp. 173–78, where she discusses "tragic choices" similar to those discussed in this book.

Page 30: Model Penal Code. Drafted during the late 1950s, the Official Draft appeared in 1962, and was prepared and published by the American Law Institute, Philadelphia, Pennsylvania. Since then the Code has served as a baseline against which to measure possible and proposed reforms in American procedural and substantive criminal law. Most of the Code is reprinted in Sanford H. Kadish, Stephen J. Schulhofer, and Monrad G. Paulsen, eds., *Criminal Law and Its Processes*, 4th ed., Boston, Little, Brown, 1983, pp. xlvii–cxvi.

Page 30: Choose the Lesser Evil. For a discussion of this principle as a mode of justification (not excuse) in the criminal law, see Fletcher, *Rethinking the Criminal Law*, pp. 774–98; and Kadish, Schulhofer, and Paulson, *Criminal Law and Its Processes* (in which necessity and choice of the lesser evil are discussed together).

Page 30: James Fitzjames Stephen. The passage quoted comes from his *Digest of the Criminal Law,* 5th ed., London, Macmillan, 1894, p. 25, n. 1. The passage quoted from Stephens on p. 33 appears in his *History of the Criminal Law of England,* 3 vols., London, Macmillan, 1883, vol. 2, p. 108.

Page 30: Benjamin N. Cardozo. The passage quoted comes from his *Law and Literature,* New York, Harcourt Brace, 1931, p. 113. His position against the excuse of necessity is fundamentally the same as that of Cahn, *The Moral Decision.*

Page 33: utilitarian thinking. Utilitarianism plays a prominent role in my discussion in chapter 3; see pp. 73–79.

Page 33: the Constitution is not a "suicide pact." The phrase appears in *Kennedy v. Mendoza-Martinez,* 372 U.S. 144 (1963), at p. 160, in the opinion for the Court by Justice Arthur J. Goldberg.

CHAPTER TWO

Page 44: speluncean explorers. Lon Fuller published "The Case of the Speluncean Explorers" in *The Harvard Law Review,* vol. 62, 1949, pp. 616–45; at about the same time, he published it in his casebook *The Problems of Jurisprudence,* temp. ed., Brooklyn, Foundation Press, 1949, pp. 1–27. There are some slight differences between the two versions. In subsequent years it has been reprinted, in whole or in part, in many places, e.g., in *An Introduction to Law,* a volume prepared by the editors of the *Harvard Law Review,* Cambridge, 1968, pp. 20–49; and most recently in Joel Feinberg and Hyman Gross, eds., *The Philosophy of Law,* 5th ed., Belmont, Cal., Wadsworth, 1995, pp. 535–49. The only published discussion of the case of which I am aware is by

Anthony D'Amato, "The Speluncean Explorers—Further Proceedings," *Stanford Law Review,* 32 (Winter, 1980), 467–85, reprinted in Feinberg and Gross, *The Philosophy of Law,* pp. 549–53.

Page 45: Regina v. Dudley and Stephens. Probably the most famous lifeboat case involving murder and cannibalism, tried in England in 1884 and reported in Q.B.D. [Queen's Bench Division], vol. 14, starting at p. 273. The case is a classic and has been much discussed (e.g., by Simpson, *Cannibalism and the Common Law*) and reprinted (e.g., it is excerpted in Kadish, Schulhofer, and Paulson, *Criminal Law and Its Processes,* pp. 182–86).

Page 46: law on necessity. This defense in the criminal law is discussed, e.g., by George P. Fletcher, *Rethinking the Criminal Law,* Boston, Little, Brown, 1978, pp. 818–29; and by Kadish, Schulhofer, and Paulson, *Criminal Law and Its Processes,* pp. 769–88 (who treat necessity as a justification, not as an excuse); and Smith and Hogan, *Criminal Law,* pp. 191–99.

Page 47: self-defense. The subject is discussed in a fascinating case study by George P. Fletcher, *A Crime of Self-Defense: Bernhard Goetz and the Law on Trial,* New York, Free Press, 1988. See also Suzanne Uniacke, *Permissible Killing: The Self-Defense Justification in Homicide,* Cambridge, Cambridge University Press, 1994.

Page 62: right to life. Affirmation of such a right far exceeds analysis of what this right consists in. I discussed it in "The Right to Life," *The Monist,* 52 (October 1968), pp. 550–72; so have several others, e.g., Franciszek Przetacznik, "The Right to Life as a Basic Human Right," *Revue de droit international,* 56 (Janvier–Mars 1973), pp. 23–47, and in his subsequent essay of the same title in *Revue des droits de l'homme,* 9 (1976), pp. 585–608; H. J. McCloskey, "The Right to Life," *Mind,* 84 (1975), pp. 403–25; George P. Fletcher, "The Right to Life," *Georgia Law Review,* 13 (Summer 1979), pp. 1371–94; B. G. Ramcharan, ed., *The Right to Life in International Law,* Dordrecht, Martinus Nijhoff, 1985; and my review in *Law and Philosophy,* vol. 7 (1988), pp. 237–45.

Page 50: Hobbes's Principle. Hobbes writes: "[H]e that does anything by the authority from another does therein no injury to him by whose authority he acts," since "to do injury to one's self is impossible." *Leviathan,* ed. Richard Tuck, Cambridge, Cambridge University Press, 1991, Pt. II, ch. 18, p. 124.

Page 51: Locke on rights. See Locke's second *Treatise,* sections 6, 23, 85, 135, and 168, and in *Two Treatises of Government,* ed. Peter Laslett, Cambridge, Cambridge University Press, 1960.

Page 53: Shirley Jackson, "The Lottery." Jackson's famous essay was first published in the *New Yorker* in 1948 and has been widely reprinted, e.g., in Sylvan Barnet, ed., *The Harper Anthology of Fiction,* New York, Harper Collins, 1991, pp. 862–68. I am indebted to my colleague, Sylvan Barnet, for this reference.

Page 55: Contractual considerations. See, e.g., E. Allen Farnsworth, *Farnsworth on Contracts,* 3 vols., Boston, Little, Brown, 1990, vol. 2, pp. 61–69.

Page 58: utilitarianism. Versions and discussions of utilitarianism abound. Apart from the classic writings of Jeremy Bentham, J. S. Mill, Henry Sidgwick, and G. E. Moore, perhaps the most widely discussed recent version of utilitarianism is by J. J. C. Smart; it appears in Smart and Bernard Williams, *Utilitarianism For and Against,* Cambridge, Cambridge University Press, 1973; see also Antony Quinton, *Utilitarian Ethics,* London, Macmillan, 1973; 2nd ed, La Salle, Ill., Open Court, 1989. An anthology of recent criticism will be found in Samuel Scheffler, ed., *Consequentialism and Its Critics,* New York, Oxford University Press, 1988.

Page 58: transplant case. See the discussion in Thomson, *The Realm of Rights,* pp. 135–48.

Page 65: cannibalism in the Andes. Alive: The Story of the Andes Survivors, by Piers Paul Read, was published in Philadelphia by J. B. Lippincott in 1974. The discussion among the survivors leading up to their decision to eat the flesh of those who died in the airplane crash will be found on pp. 81–84.

Page 67: neither victims nor executioners. Albert Camus used this phrase (or rather Dwight Macdonald, his English translator, did) as the title of an essay originally published in the now-defunct journal *Politics,* July–August 1947. I first read it as reprinted in the likewise now-defunct journal *Liberation,* February 1960, pp. 4–10. New Society Publishers, Philadelphia, reprinted the essay as a booklet in 1986 for the Resource Center for Nonviolence, Santa Cruz, California.

CHAPTER THREE

Page 72: Jim and the Indians. The case as I quote it appeared originally in Smart and Williams, *Utilitarianism For and Against,* pp. 98–99. Williams's use of the case to argue against utilitarian moral reasoning is the target of an amusing essay (allegedly from Jim's memoirs some years later) by Martin Hollis, "Jim and the Indians," *Analysis* 43 (1983), pp. 36–39.

Page 73: Sophie's Choice. William Styron's novel of this

title was published in New York by Random House in 1979. The story of Sophie's choice is told on pp. 483–84.

Page 78: John Stuart Mill and rule utilitarianism. The phrase "rule utilitarianism" became popular in the 1950s; the idea, if not the phrase, is clearly and influentially to be found in J. O. Urmson, "The Interpretation of the Moral Philosophy of J. S. Mill," *Philosophical Quarterly,* 3 (January 1953), pp. 33–39, reprinted in Michael D. Bayles, *Contemporary Utilitarianism,* New York, Doubleday, Anchor Books, 1968. As Urmson correctly points out, Mill advises us to rely on what he called "secondary principles," such as "Do not tell lies," for everyday moral choices, and he counseled appeal to the principle of utility itself only where such principles were in conflict, or were in need of fundamental revision on utilitarian grounds, or where there was no recognized secondary principle relevant to the problem of moral choice at hand.

Page 79: murder. The Model Penal Code declares "[a] person [to be] guilty of criminal homicide if he purposely, knowingly, recklessly, or negligently causes the death of another human being" (sec. 210.1); there is no important difference beween this definition of homicide and the Code's later definition of murder. This is at considerable variance with most American law, which contrasts first- and second-degree murder and distinguishes both from voluntary manslaughter, and the traditional definition of murder in English law, according to which any "unlawful" homicide is murder provided it is done "with malice aforethought"; see Kadish, Schulhofer, and Paulson, *Criminal Law and Its Processes,* p. 408. Despite appearances to the contrary, Jim's killing an Indian would be murder under the latter definition (because of the way "malice" is defined) just as it would be murder under the Model Penal Code.

Page 82: duress. The quotation is from Kadish, Schulhofer, and Paulson, *Criminal Law and Its Processes,* p. 792. See also Smith and Hogan, *Criminal Law,* pp. 199–209.

Page 83: Doctrine of Double Effect. In the text I have formulated this principle after the manner suggested by Tom L. Beauchamp, "Suicide," in Tom Regan, ed., *Matters of Life and Death,* 3rd ed., New York, McGraw-Hill, 1993, p. 89. The principle has been a staple of Catholic moral philosophy; interest in it generally by philosophers was the result of the discussion by Philippa Foot, "The Problem of Abortion and the Doctrine of Double Effect" (1967), reprinted in her *Virtues and Vices and Other Essays in Moral Philosophy,* Berkeley and Los Angeles, University of California Press, 1978, pp. 19–32.

Page 87: Austin on "if". The reference is to the paper by J. L. Austin, "What Sort of 'If' is the 'If' in "I can if I choose'?", published in *Analysis* 12 (June 1952), pp. 125–26, but not reprinted in his *Philosophical Papers.*

Page 88: killing versus letting die. Whether there is any moral significance in the difference between acts describable as "killing" in contrast to acts describable as "letting die" has spawned a considerable literature. The discussion seems to have been initiated by Jonathan Bennett, "Acting and Refraining," *Analysis,* 28 (1967), pp. 30–31; a useful anthology on both practical and theoretical aspects of the controversy is by Bonnie Steinbock, ed., *Killing and Letting Die,* Englewood Cliffs, N.J., Prentice-Hall, 1980. Perhaps the most persistent arguments against any moral significance in the distinction are those by James Rachels; see his *The End of Life,* Oxford, Oxford University Press, 1986.

Page 83: Numbers: Do they matter? Contemporary discussion of this problem can be partly tracked through John M. Taurek, "Should the Numbers Count?" *Philosophy and Public Affairs,* 6 (Summer 1977), pp. 293–316; Derek Parfit, "Innumerate Ethics," *Philosophy and Public Affairs,* 7 (Summer 1978), pp. 285–301; and John T. Sanders, "Why the Numbers Should Sometimes Count," *Philosophy and Public Affairs,* 17 (Winter 1988), pp. 3–14.

Page 90: Trolley Problem. Invented by Philippa Foot, "The Problem of Abortion and the Doctrine of Double Effect," p. 23, one of the best subsequent discussions will be found in Thomson, *The Realm of Rights,* pp. 176–202.

Page 94: consent to one's own death. The issue has been most extensively discussed in connection with physician-assisted suicide and euthanasia. The proposition that suitably informed and verified voluntary consent to one's own assisted death justifies the one who assists and therefore nullifies any charge of murder is implicitly accepted by some writers, e.g., James Rachels, *The End of Life,* and (of course) by Dr. Jack Kevorkian, who has made physician-assisted suicide a household phrase; see his *Prescription: Medicide,* Buffalo, N.Y., Prometheus, 1991, pp. 192–93.

Page 95: Duty and "ought." At least since P. H. Nowell-Smith's book, *Ethics* (1954), philosophers have labored to convince others that the concepts of obligation, of duty, and of what we ought to do are best kept distinct. For a recent effort in this vein, see Thomson, *The Realm of Rights,* pp. 61–104.

Page 95: mechanical morality and algorithms. Elsewhere I have offered a sketch of what a morality algorithm might look like and why we should be skeptical about whether any such decision-making procedure is on the horizon; see "Ethical Decision Making and a Primitive Model of Rules," *Philosophical Topics,* 14 (Fall 1986), pp. 117–29.

Page 96: Jesus' words. They appear twice in the Bible, first in Matthew 26:42 and again in Mark 14:36.

Index